CW00763072

STEVE MALONEY

NORFOLK BROADS CANOE AND KAYAK GUIDE

Important notice – disclaimer

Canoeing and kayaking are healthy outdoor activities that carry some degree of risk. They involve adventurous travel, often away from close habitation. Guidebooks give an idea of where to access the water, where to egress, the level of difficulty and the nature of the hazards to be encountered.

However, nature being what it is, river valleys are changed by time and erosion, water levels vary considerably with rain, and constructed features can be updated or altered. This guidebook is no substitute for personal inspection at the time of paddling, and your own risk assessment and judgement. Your decision to paddle or not, and any consequences arising from that decision, is your responsibility.

Alcohol and water are a potentially lethal combination and the wonderful pubs listed in this guide should be enjoyed responsibly. Alcoholic beverages are best enjoyed after the day's watersports activities are over.

Second Edition 2020

First published in Great Britain 2016 by Pesda Press
Tan y Coed Canol
Ceunant
Caernarfon
Gwynedd
LL55 4RN

Copyright © 2016/2020 Steve Maloney

ISBN: 978-1-906095-73-8

The Author asserts the moral right to be identified as the author of this work.

All rights reserved. No part of this publication may be reproduced, stored in a retrieval system, or transmitted, in any form or by any means, electronic, mechanical, photocopying, recording or otherwise, without the prior written permission of the Publisher.

Printed in Poland, lfbookservices.co.uk

Dedication

For Dad. Thank you for always being interested and encouraging. For giving me the love of adventure. And because now I understand how good it feels to be proud of your children.

Contents

CONTENTS

The Author

So here we are, a good few years and many paddled miles after I started researching the first edition of the Canoe and Kayak Guide. It's great to see increasing numbers of people out there enjoying the wonderful Broads area by canoe or kayak and having so much fun in a more environmentally sustainable way. My family and I still love to get out on The Broads and even now are able to find new waters we have yet to explore fully, while on our favourite stretches there is always something new to see. The overwhelmingly positive response to the first edition of the guide book was wonderful and I sincerely hope that the updates in this new version help even more people to get out there and make the most of the amazing natural resource we have in the Norfolk Broads.

Photographs

All photographs by Steve Maloney, except where acknowledged in the captions.

Introduction

Things have changed a great deal since I started out paddling, and with so much choice available, a little time spent chatting and some honest advice can go a long way. Working in a canoe and kayak store, I found that once a customer had decided upon and paid for their shiny new boat, invariably the next question would be, "Great, now where's a good place to paddle around here?"

With paddling on and around the Broads becoming ever more popular, I found myself being asked this more and more often. Alternatively, people would come in with tales of where they had tried to get on the water and were subsequently accosted by a local politely telling them to clear off.

It was this that initially made me start researching safe places to launch and land. Living so close to so much water that is perfect for paddling I feel it is a terrible waste if you don't use it. The Broads is a unique wetland environment, with spectacular wildlife and scenery that is ideal for exploring by canoe or kayak. It is underused by paddlers, and simply talking to people about the various different waterways makes me want to grab a boat and get out there.

I love to paddle about on the Broads at a relaxed pace, watching the wildlife and scenery, being hassled by the ducks and swans as they try to steal my sandwiches, ducking to avoid a low-flying kingfisher, or chucking a rod over the side and having a go at giving some maggots a wash. I had my favourite areas to paddle, but I soon found myself coming up with the same questions I was being asked in the shop. Finding places to launch a canoe or kayak around the Broads can prove to be more than a little difficult, with many places being under the control of a local parish council that may have restrictions in place as to who can and cannot use the facilities. So I decided that I would do the research and try to create the definitive guide. Little did I know what I was letting myself in for. But a couple of years down the road and a good few paddling miles later and here we are. My hope is that this guidebook helps paddlers use the Broads and encourages more people to take to the water and start their own love affair with paddling.

Horsey Mill Windpump, River Thurne.

The Norfolk Broads

Situated across the two counties of Norfolk and Suffolk, the Broads is undoubtedly one of the most picturesque and varied wetland landscapes in the country, and is the only wetland environment to be granted national park status in the UK. With over 120 miles of water navigable by boat, and so much more available to canoes and kayaks, the Norfolk Broads represents a vast and still relatively untapped destination for paddlers.

The Broads

The Broads themselves are pits that were formed as a result of peat digging during the Middle Ages that later flooded. Dotted along the rivers you will see windmills that were originally constructed to pump water out of the peat bogs to keep the low-lying fields from flooding and so open to agriculture. The majority of the actual broads are found in the northern part of the area. Many are close to the main rivers and easily accessed with signposted channels off the rivers. Some are small and set some distance away from the river making it impossible to get to them, while others are private and closed off to the public. The fourteen broads that are accessible to the paddler vary in size. The smallest is perfect for a short session and the largest can take several hours to explore fully.

The rivers

The rivers that traverse the Broads area vary from reed-lined stretches of straight, open water to narrow winding tributaries framed by overhanging trees and secret backwater inlets. Some sections of the rivers are extremely busy throughout the summer months and can be quite a challenge to navigate due to the boat traffic.

Being a favourite holiday destination, the summer months see the more popular parts of the Broads filled with large, multiple-berth cruisers hired out to the public. In particular, along the busier stretches of the Bure around Wroxham and Horning you will find them jostling for position at staithes (a staithe is a landing stage for boats) and attempting to moor up. Remember that many of the people driving these boats are on holiday and have little experience of manoeuvring such large craft. Staying clear of this particular stretch of the Bure in the summer, or at least being aware of and prepared for some dubious piloting skills, is a good idea. Don't let this put you off though, as thankfully these sections are generally quite wide and it is possible to keep fairly close in to the bank and out of harm's way. More often the paddler only needs to traverse these sections for a short distance in order to access calmer waters away from traffic. The majority of local paddlers will give these areas a wide berth throughout the holiday period and seek out quieter sections of river. Indeed, other parts of the smaller rivers and broads are completely inaccessible to motorised craft and provide extremely peaceful and rewarding summertime paddling.

Something for everyone

If you take your time there are many little inlets and secret coves to really bring out the adventurer in you and the family; or find yourself a little piece of paradise and get away from it all. For many, paddling on the Broads is their first experience of recreation on the water and it often leads to a lifetime passion for watersports and exploration.

For the kayak fisherman the Broads area represents a fantastic opportunity to find the kind of swims that those restricted to the banks can only dream of. Superb days of fishing can be had, and the ability to head off into waters that appear never to have been fished can deliver some truly thrilling days out.

Canoes and kayaks are generally unthreatening to resident wildlife, which is consequently much less timid. This regularly offers the paddler superb views of usually shy and reclusive creatures. Kingfishers, owls, harriers and even the famous bittern can all be seen, along with a wide variety of dragonflies, damselflies and of course our beautiful swallowtail butterfly. Otters and water voles are not uncommon in certain stretches, along with pike and swimming grass snakes as they warm themselves basking in the summer sun.

Both amateur and professional photographers will appreciate the varied views and vistas offered by the Broads landscape, while the ability to get up close and personal to the wildlife can deliver some truly remarkable pictures and memories.

Whatever your paddling preference, be it touring, fishing, picnicking, photography, wildlife or even just people watching from one of the many waterside pubs, there is certainly a part of the Broads to suit your needs.

Area covered

This guide covers the waterways that make up the Broads area and the section of the Waveney from Harleston to Bungay that is covered by an access agreement which is well worth exploring. To paddle on the Broads you will need to have either a British Canoeing /Canoe England licence or a Broads Authority Licence. An overview of the different options is listed opposite.

Broads Authority Licence

- One licence required for each boat that you paddle.
- Valid from 1st April to 31st March.
- Licence covers Broads Authority area only.
- Contact the Tolls Office for prices or visit their website.
- Short visit tolls are also available for periods of 1–7 days and 8–14 days.

Tolls can be obtained from the Broads Authority Tolls Office directly at 62–64 Thorpe Road, Norwich, NR1 1RY.

British Canoeing / Canoe England Membership

- Covers 5000km of British Waterways including the Broads area.
- Licenses the person not the boat, so allows flexibility if you change canoe or kayak.
- Valid for 12 months from date of purchase.
- Access to members' area of website.
- Four digital editions of Canoe Focus magazine.
- Includes 3rd party liability insurance up to £10 million.

British Canoeing membership can be obtained online at www.britishcanoeing.org.uk or you can call them on 0300 0119500. Family and life memberships are also available.

Remember to carry your licence card with you when out paddling!

📷 *Exiting Catfield Dyke onto Hickling Broad.*

📷 *Keeping safe on the water.*

Safety

Paddling is an assumed risk sport and while the unexpected can and does happen, risks can be minimised by taking the appropriate preparatory steps and having the right equipment. As with all watersports safety is always the priority.

Be sure to have the right kit with you: appropriate clothing for the weather conditions and water temperature, good buoyancy aid, knife and first aid kit, whistle and a means of contacting the emergency services if required with your accurate location. If that means is a phone, be sure to keep it on you and waterproof! Aquapacs are a great idea as they are completely waterproof and you can use your phone while it is still in the case; you don't have to take it out. Other items that may be advisable are: VHF radio, spare paddle, change of clothing, towel, sunscreen and hat, food and drink, waterproof watch, hand-operated bilge pump or sponge, waterproof dry bags and map case.

Try not to paddle alone. Paddling is generally a social pastime and it can be a lot more fun sharing the experience. However, if you do venture out solo, tell someone where you are going and when you expect to be back. Just remember to let them know you have safely made it back, or they may not speak to you again for giving them the fright of their lives and making them call out the emergency services!

Emergency services

The Norfolk Broads has its own contacts that deal with emergencies and some policing.

Broads Control

Broads Control is staffed by experienced waterways officers and is equipped with VHF, computer links and phone lines allowing them to effectively liaise with the coastguard, police and Environment Agency. The Broads Controller can be reached on 01603 756056 or VHF channel 12.

Broads Beat

Broads Beat is a Norfolk Constabulary initiative that patrols the Broads area and can be contacted between the hours of 9am – 6pm during summer and 9am-5pm during winter. The Broads Beat team deal with any river-based situation from theft through to anti-social behaviour, and work closely with the Broads Authority. They can be contacted on 101.

Contacts:

Broads Control
01603 756056 or VHF channel 12
Broads Beat
Call 101 Ext 1235 or 1236

Making friends at Rockland Broad.

Remember:

- Check the weather and tide times for the day of your trip and plan your clothing and equipment accordingly.
- Carry a means of communication with you (e.g. mobile phone).
- Where possible don't paddle alone and if you have to, make sure someone knows where you are going. If your plans change, give them a call to let them know and tell them when you are back safe.
- Look out for large motor cruisers and other craft. As paddlers we're not very visible when there are boats overtaking each other on the wider rivers, or coming around tight corners on the narrower stretches of rivers. Also remember that sailing craft have the right of way.

Swans at Potter Heigham, River Thurne.

Access and Environmental Issues

The Broads are a unique environment, and so as paddlers we need to do our part to ensure that it remains that way. At all times we should be considerate towards the environment and other water users.

Bio-security on the Broads

Currently the area is under attack from a couple of invasive species that need to be controlled. Being aware of the different types of flora and fauna that are causing concern, and knowing how to prevent their spread, will help win the fight.

The killer shrimp – *Dikerogammarus villosus*

This aggressively invasive species of shrimp originates from Eastern Europe. It kills a number of our native aquatic fauna including small fish and can grow up to 30mm in length. The Broads Authority has been working hard to get the message about the killer shrimp out there, and to get paddlers to take action with the 'Check, Clean and Dry' campaign. Keep an eye out for the extensive signage and information boards at launching points and take the time to read them. Many paddlers like to explore different areas and as such we are the shrimps' perfect partners. If you use your gear regularly, please check it and wash it down after every outing to help prevent the spread. Any kit you have used should also be thoroughly dried, the shrimps can live for up to two weeks in moist conditions.

Himalayan balsam

This fast-growing and even faster-spreading plant with its attractive pinky-purple flowers, pungent odour, and explosive seed pods, which can launch their contents up to five metres, is fast becoming a real scourge of our waterways. It crowds out our native flora and can block small waterways completely in only a couple of years.

Access

Although this book has been written in good faith and the information is accurate at the time of writing, access agreements to the water can change. It is only through responsible paddling that we can ensure the continuation and improvement of access for this wonderful pastime in areas as beautiful as the Broads. If you happen to come into contact with locals or other river users while you are out, chat to them! If we are considerate, friendly and open about our sport, not only will we keep the places where we can launch, but we may just acquire a few more in the process.

For the latest information on access to the Broads, contact either the Broads Authority or British Canoeing's River Access Officer.

Locks Inn, River Waveney.

Remember:

- Follow the Countryside Code.
- Keep to designated launching points and don't seal launch. Try not to drag boats over banks etc. and keep erosion to a minimum.
- Take only photographs and leave only footprints (or ripples).
- Follow navigation rules and stay on the right-hand side of the waterway where possible.
- Many of the small waterways and dykes that join the rivers and broads may be privately owned. If there are signs stating 'Private' and 'No Access', or if there is a rope or chain preventing entry, please respect this and do not enter. It will be restricted for a good reason. Sometimes local landowners hold shoots that can be close to the water, so please be careful.
- Keep your boat and kit clean. There is a particularly nasty foreign shrimp trying to get into the Broads at the moment and we need to help control its spread. See the section Bio-security on the Broads.

📷 *Crayfish.*

Contacts

Broads Authority
Yare House
62–64 Thorpe Road
Norwich
Norfolk
NR1 1RY
01603 610734
www.broads-authority.gov.uk

British Canoeing
National Water Sports Centre
Adbolton Lane
Holme Pierrepont
Nottingham
NG12 2LU
0300 0119500
Email: info@britishcanoeing.org.uk
www.britishcanoeing.org.uk
www.go-canoeing.org

Horsey Mere Thatcher's Cottage, River Thurne.

How to Use this Guide

The information contained within this guide is intended to satisfy as many different types of paddler as possible. Whether you are using a canoe, kayak, sit-on-top or inflatable, are out for just a day or touring the entire Broads region, you should be able to find both launching points and trip details to suit your level and requirements. For a first time paddle, it may be advisable to stick to the quieter parts of the Broads where there are no motorised craft. This is safer and less intimidating, and your initial paddle will hopefully be more enjoyable and leave you wanting more.

The list of launching places in this guide is fairly comprehensive, and the 'Table of Launching Points' provides an easy 'at a glance' reference which should enable you to quickly narrow down and select your starting and finishing locations.

Selecting your launching point and trip

Most launching places on the Broads have free parking close to the water; however these areas can often have limited spaces. Other spots are mainly pay and display but usually have very reasonable all-day rates. Be aware that some parking areas are signposted for parishioners only, and in certain villages you may be afforded a very vocal 'welcome' from someone, if you turn up with a boat on your roof.

The majority of canoe and kayak launching points on the Broads involve a bankside, small vertical drop to the water level of usually around 50cm. These kinds of launches are easier for canoes and sit-on-tops, but kayaks take a little more practice. Some locations may also have slipways; however many of these are for the use of parishioners and locals only whereas others have a small charge or donation to use them. The Broads Authority (BA) is currently working hard to encourage paddlesports and this involves the upgrading of many launch points, however if you do find

📷 *Family fun on Rockland Broad.*

damage, or a site that is in need of repair, the BA will be only too happy to hear from you. Many of the boatyards throughout the Broads may allow you to park your car and launch a boat using their facilities; it is simply a matter of asking their permission. All of this information is provided in this guide.

The rivers are mostly very slow flowing, but some stretches are affected by tidal forces and can be quite fast and thus increase the duration of your trip, or restrict access altogether. Other sections can be extremely weedy with very narrow channels or shallow areas that may have you practising your poling skills. We don't exactly have a great deal of whitewater in Norfolk, and with the land being so flat there are hardly any locks to contend with, so having to portage your boat around an obstacle in the Broads area is fairly rare, with the exception of the Waveney where there are a couple of portages and potentially the occasional fallen tree to look out for. It all adds to the adventure.

Generally the Broads is a pretty safe area to paddle, with few hazards except for other craft. As long as you are aware of what is going on around you, and keep an eye out for the inexperienced and unexpected, everything should be fine.

Waypoints

The Broads covers a vast area and there is the possibility of some very long days out or even overnight trips. Breaking up a trip can make it that bit more enjoyable, and to help with this not only are there launching points listed in this guide, but you will also find Broads Authority 24-hour moorings dotted around the rivers. These are generally small, grassy areas that make ideal picnic spots. Many of the waypoints have picnic tables or benches that make them perfect for families to break up their adventure and pause for a rest.

Access to these places is on a first come first served basis, so be aware that on arrival you may find that there is no space for you to land as cruisers have moored up. The bank level at some of these moorings can be around a metre high, however if that is the case there should be a little ladder built into the pilings that you can use to help get in and out of your boat.

As you paddle around you will find that there are many places to simply pull out or moor up against and have a breather. One item I have found to be most useful at places like these is a length of floating rope or a throw line. This you can use to secure your boat and stop any embarrassing mishaps as you gracefully exit your cockpit onto the ladder or bank only to see your boat slowly drifting away. There speaks the voice of experience!

Also included in the guide is a list of the riverside pubs you can visit. There are a number of riverside campsites within the Broads, but these are fairly few and mostly spread around the southern part of the area. However they do add real adventure if you are coming to the Broads on a paddling and camping holiday.

Distance charts

Each river has a dedicated chart with details of the distances from one launching point to another. From these it should be possible to work out a fairly accurate total distance for any paddle trip between launching places or waypoints, and an approximate duration for that trip. Distances within the data charts are given in kilometres; if you prefer to work in miles then simply divide by 1.6.

Tides

For the majority of paddlers, high tide will have minimal effect, but for those paddlers wanting to explore further, it can be very important. Wherever you are planning to paddle it is still a good idea to check because in instances of very high tides, the tidal range can be up to 2m and make paddling far more challenging. Tidal range is the difference between the height of high and low water.

Tidal information

By checking the tidal data for Gorleston and then the 'High Tide Times around the Broads' spreadsheet you can work out when high tide will hit the area of the Broads you are paddling. You can find the Gorleston Tide Tables online or buy a booklet from a fishing tackle shop or a yacht chandlers.

Above all: be safe, go prepared and have fun.

Rockland Broad, River Yare.

The Rivers and their Associated Broads

Although there are seven rivers that make their way through the Broads, the majority of the accessible broads themselves are found in the northern part of the area off the rivers Bure, Ant and Thurne. While some of the broads form almost a part of the river itself, many are set slightly away from the rivers and are connected via a short channel. Throughout the summer months some sections of the main rivers can be extremely busy with boat traffic, whereas some of the broads have areas and channels that are only accessible to a canoe or kayak. These broads offer superb places to get away from the tug boats and can be a real thrill to explore.

There are seven rivers that make their way through the Broads area:

- The Bure
- The Ant
- The Thurne
- The Wensum (a tributary of the Yare)
- The Yare
- The Chet
- The Waveney

Broads that are accessible to the paddler are:

- Bridge Broad (Bure)
- Wroxham Broad (Bure)
- Salhouse Broad (Bure)
- Hoveton Little Broad (Black Horse Broad) (Bure)*
- Malthouse Broad (Bure)
- South Walsham Broad (Bure)
- Barton Broad (Ant)
- Sutton Broad (Ant)
- Hickling Broad (Thurne)
- Horsey Mere (Thurne)**
- Surlingham Broad / Bargate (Yare)
- Rockland Broad (Yare)
- Oulton Broad (Waveney)

*Access to Hoveton Little Broad is seasonal and it cannot be paddled between 31st October and the first Saturday of the Spring Bank Holiday.

** Horsey Mere is a winter wildfowl refuge and access is not permitted between 1st November and 1st March.

The rivers

River Bure

The River Bure enters the Broads area at **Horstead Mill** close to the little village of Coltishall. Well known for the ruins of its mill, Horstead is a very popular spot with local paddlers. There has been a mill here since Saxon times with the last incarnation being destroyed by fire in January 1963, during a winter so harsh that the fire engines in attendance had to cut through more than a foot of ice to reach water and put out the blaze.

Here the Bure offers paddlers some small taste of whitewater as it flows from the old mill races into the mill pool. It's not exactly the River Dart, but it does present an opportunity for anyone in the area wanting to experience faster flowing water without having to travel a great distance. Launching into the flowing water of the mill pool can be tricky for first timers; however there is the option of a nice, calm, easy entry using the slipway into the still water by the lock on the other side of the mill. Once you've launched and are paddling downstream from the lock, you move silently beneath the overhanging arms of the trees and pass a few old moorings, where the boats range from nice, clean and well-loved small cruisers to moss-covered and neglected hulks sinking slowly into the water. There has been some work here recently to shore up the bank and build new moorings with access to the Norfolk Mead Hotel, a beautiful former Georgian merchant's house which is

Horstead Mill launching.

now a luxurious bed and breakfast and also excellent restaurant. Joining from the right is the access to the faster-flowing mill stream. If you choose to paddle up this little stretch, you pass through the gardens of a particularly fine house as you approach the mill pool, so please keep this in mind and be courteous.

This part of the river from the lock to Coltishall Common is relatively quiet and a great place to enjoy quiet paddling and watch the wildlife. Motor boats generally stop at Coltishall Common and come no further, so it's a good place to paddle and gain some confidence. As you approach Coltishall Common you see the Rising Sun pub and then the long moorings. If you are in need of a break already then both the Rising Sun and Kings Head offer a good selection of food and drink and mooring up at the staithe is usually quite easy. There is also a very large grassy area which is perfect for picnics. If you are paddling from Wroxham this can be a great place to stop and refresh before the return paddle.

📷 *Coltishall Common.*

Alternatively if the staithe is busy, continue on to **Belaugh Staithe (2)** which has a little slipway recently improved by the Broads Authority, which now makes landing and launching much easier. Passing the little village of Belaugh you will see the church of St Peter high up on the hill, which was a favourite of the famous poet and writer Sir John Betjeman. The Bure then winds its way through some beautiful scenery, with the river surrounded by oaks and alders as it works its way towards Wroxham, the Heart of the Broads. As you approach Wroxham you will see an entrance on your right that leads to the small Bridge Broad. You can paddle into this channel, explore the broad and exit via a smaller channel right next to the Wroxham railway bridge and the next launch point.

Hoveton Riverside Park (3) in the Roys long term car park provides an unexpectedly picturesque and peaceful setting from which to launch. It features a large decked area surrounded by trees and a small arched foot-bridge that is more reminiscent of Japanese willow pattern than the Norfolk Broads. Alternatively if you are stopping for a break, then the public staithe on your left just before the bridge can be a good place to pull up. This landing spot is right next to the King's Head pub, local shops and even a chippy. Throughout the summer months this area certainly beats to the sounds of hire craft. The road bridge here was built in 1619 replacing a much earlier one, and as such it can be tricky for the bigger boats to get through. Many boatyards that hire out craft are based here, so paddlers beware of first time captains, especially as you head under the bridge.

As you paddle through the hustle and bustle of Wroxham you pass some of the most desirable waterside properties on the Broads. Indeed there have been a number of famous residents here including the entertainer George Formby.

Paddling away from Wroxham you come first to the larger **Wroxham Broad (4)** and then a little further on is delightful **Salhouse Broad (5)** with its picturesque beach that is ideal for easy landings and a picnic. Overnight camping can now be arranged at Salhouse Broad so it makes this venue great for anyone planning a multi-day expedition. Salhouse is a very popular place for beginners to paddle around and explore. There is plenty to see and it is a very safe location in which to explore, with even the challenge of finding the wreck of a First World War gunboat that can still be seen. Both of these broads are great places to paddle and escape the traffic, although Wroxham Broad is home to a sailing club and can on occasion be busy with small sailing craft. In the summer time keep your eyes peeled and ears open for the little ice cream boat that cruises the area and can be readily flagged down to provide a refreshing cone or ice lolly. A little further on from Salhouse Broad you

reach Hoveton Little Broad, also known as Black Horse Broad, just before Horning village. Hoveton Little Broad is open between Whitsunday and the 30th October each year. Interestingly, the one-time private water broad was once the scene of a rebellious mass trespass designed to re-open this water to the public. Hoveton Little Broad had a barrier across its entrance erected by the landowner but Herbert Woods, a local boat builder, led a group that dismantled the barrier in order to assert their historic right of access. This successfully resulted in the landowner granting access, if only for a short time throughout the year.

The village of **Horning (6)** is very popular and as such can be difficult for paddlers to launch from in peak season. The name Horning actually means 'folk who live on the high ground between the rivers' and the village dates back 1,000 years. Parking in the village is limited and launching can be tricky as the staithes

Salhouse Broad Beach.

📷 *Horning Ferry Staithe.*

are usually busy with cruisers. However, it is possible to get out onto the water here, and Horning provides a great place from which to explore upstream towards Salhouse Broad and Wroxham, or downstream to Malthouse and South Walsham Broads. It is also home to the impressive *Southern Comfort* Mississippi paddle boat. For those with a literary interest, the staithe at Horning is the starting point for both the *Coot Club* and *The Big Six* novels in Arthur Ransome's *Swallows and Amazons* series of children's adventure stories. Indeed this stretch of the Bure features heavily throughout both these books.

As you pass through Horning you come to the ferry which takes people across the Bure from the Woodbastwick side to the Ferry Inn and Horning itself. The Ferry Inn sits right on the waterside with a long mooring and is a perfect place to stop for lunch or a break on a day out. On the southern bank is **Woodbastwick Staithe (7)** which provides a great location for launching with a nice little gravelly beach close to the car park. This can be a good place to launch in the summer when Horning itself can be rather busy, however the access road can flood quite deeply at some peak tides so check before you go.

Around a kilometre on from Horning Ferry you pass St Benedict's Church with its impressive vicarage on your left. There is a small mooring here should you wish to have a brief stop off and visit the church. Just beyond on the southern side of the river is the entrance to **Malthouse Broad (8)**. Both the channel and broad can be busy during peak months but the broad can be a good place to take a break, with a large grassy area on your left as you enter the broad itself. There may be a small charge payable to land here, but it is a less busy option than trying to land at the staithe. If you want to stop at the information centre then aim for the little inlet just in front of the building on the far side of the broad.

📷 *New Inn, Stokesby.*

The village of Ranworth is home to St Helen's Church, often called the 'Cathedral of the Broads' due to its position on high ground and impressive views from the tower, which is open to the public and well worth the climb. Malthouse Broad is also home to one of the many ghost stories on the Broads. As you enter Malthouse Broad from the channel you will see the entry to Ranworth Broad on your right. Access to the broad itself is not allowed, however you can stop at the moorings and visit the floating Broads Wildlife Centre which is open from Easter to October.

If you continue along the Bure passing Malthouse Broad you can turn into **South Walsham Broad (9)** which tends to be a little quieter than Malthouse with fewer big cruisers. At around a mile in length it is a great place for exploring and with a good-sized free car park and easy launching, is perfect for beginners. Opposite the entrance to South Walsham Broad the River Ant joins and here you will

The Ghost of Malthouse Broad

Brother Pacificus was a 16th-century monk based at nearby St Benet's Abbey. Brother Pacificus was rowing from the abbey daily to repair the rood screen at St Helen's and he returned home one day to discover all his fellow monks slain by troops of King Henry VIII under the reformation. He was heartbroken and lived out his days a hermit to be buried in St Helen's upon his death. It is said that he can sometimes be seen of an evening rowing his small boat across the broad with his little dog on board.

find the remains of St Benet's Abbey. There is a staithe and grassy area you can use to get out and explore the abbey, and it is well worth a visit for those with an interest in history.

A little further downstream the Bure is joined from the north by the River Thurne which gives access to Potter Heigham and Hickling Broad, and just beyond that is the entry to **Upton Dyke (10)**. This can be an ideal spot to launch from and explore this area of the Bure as it has a superb car park, picnic area and easy launching. Exploring south of here you paddle along a fairly gently-winding river rimmed with high reed beds, under the road bridge and past the Bridge Inn, and then first the village of Acle and later Stokesby.

Launching and landing is possible at **Stokesby (11)** but the current and tidal influences can be quite strong. Along this part of the river your route is guided by the impressive drainage windmills that stand looming on the banks dotting the horizon. Of the many that originally kept this wide, open area from flooding only a few remain in good condition, the rest can be seen without their sails and decaying, wrapped in the arms of ivy. This part of the Bure is better paddled by those with experience. Careful planning is advisable and an understanding of the rise and fall, current and tide times is essential. This is particularly important if you are considering passing from the Bure onto the Waveney and crossing Breydon Water to access the southern part of the Broads.

St Benet's Abbey

This was the only religious house not closed down by Henry VIII in the dissolution, and was built on the foundations of a 9th-century monastery. This iconic Norfolk landmark can present some fantastic atmospheric photograph opportunities in the early morning mists or evening sunset. Don't be fooled by the round tower that protrudes from its centre. That's an 18th-century wind pump a farmer put up to help drain the land for agriculture, not an original part of the abbey. It does leave you wondering why he had to build it there!

Once heavily fortified, although very little above-ground evidence of this now remains, the abbey resisted all attacks by the Norman conquerors, until a single monk betrayed his brothers and allowed the Normans to gain access. The monk had been promised the abbacy in return for his treachery, but instead was hung by the soldiers as a traitor once St Benet's had been taken. Now there's a lesson.

St Benet's Abbey. Photo | istockphoto.com

River Ant (including North Walsham and Dilham Canal)

Although the River Ant technically enters the Broads Authority area at Wayford Bridge, it is currently possible to paddle the first section of the Dilham canal to or from Honing Lock. Built in the early 1800's and finally opened in 1826, the North Walsham and Dilham Canal was built for transporting cargo to and from the various mills along the river as far as Antingham. Although this first stretch of the canal is narrow and weedy in summer with the occasional fallen tree to cope with, it is a beautiful stretch of water to explore. A local landowner whose ancestors part funded the construction of the canal owns and controls access and in recent times has installed a donation box for paddlers at Tonnage Bridge. So, if you do choose to paddle this stretch please be aware of this and understand that your right to paddle it is down to their permission and could change at any time. Launching from Honing Lock you are greeted by overgrown reedbeds, overhanging trees and an impres-

📷 *Smallburgh Staithe.*

sive lock currently in a state of disrepair. The narrow channel close to the parking area can be accessed with relative ease and as you paddle downstream this wild and winding waterway is delightfully picturesque and a great place to spot otters and other wildlife.

Wayford Bridge (14) is a good starting place from which to explore the canal. There are two options for launching, one on either side of the bridge. The public staithe on the southern side, known as **Smallburgh Staithe (15)**, has a maximum limit of 12 feet for the length of boats that can be launched there, while the Wayford Bridge Inn is happy for paddlers to park and launch. Out of courtesy, check with the staff before launching and nip back in for a drink or snack on your return. The hotel is a great place to start or finish your trip. It's only fair and it keeps paddlers in their good books. There has been a river crossing at Wayford Bridge for many centuries and the discovery of a hard surface across the riverbed that formed the original 'ford' is what gives the location its name. The point where the canal joins the Ant at Wayford Bridge is the limit of navigation for motorised craft which makes this little waterway ideal for canoes and kayaks. The canal heads directly north from the bridge, and the often overgrown and narrow channel winds its way to **Honing Lock (12)**, the most northerly limit of the Broads area. At Wayford Bridge you are also able to head off west towards Tyler's Cut and **Dilham Staithe (13)**. These are well worth exploring if you like a little adventure, paddling beneath arching trees and discovering forgotten inlets with a real feeling

Sutton Staithe.

Neatishead Staithe.

of entering the wilds. There is a small staithe at Dilham which makes a great place to stop and have a break before your return trip.

From Wayford Bridge the River Ant heads south for a little over a kilometre and a half, passing the beautifully restored Hunsett Mill on your left before it meets the access to Stalham and Sutton. Stalham is a centre for hiring of cruisers and this makes the river from here onwards that bit busier. Turning left at this point will take you east towards either Stalham or Sutton, and you soon come to a fork in the river where if you head left you reach Stalham, or if you head right, **Sutton Staithe (17)**.

At **Stalham Staithe (16)** you will find the Museum of the Broads where you can learn a great deal about life on the Broads throughout the past. There are moorings right by the museum so access by canoe and kayak is easy. Alternatively you can head towards Sutton across the broad and stop for a break or lunch at the hotel, which has a large grassy area in front, ideal for a picnic, and again is easily accessed by boat. If you continue south, you come to the wide, open water of Barton Broad. On approaching this particular broad, to the right you will see

the channel that leads to **Barton Turf (18)** and pass the triangular island known as 'The Heater', perhaps due to it resembling an old iron. The second largest of the Broads, Barton is a great location for spending some time paddling. Here the paddler has the option of either exploring the broad itself or heading towards **Neatishead Staithe (19)** or Irstead, both of which provide pleasant stopping points.

Tucked away on the eastern side of the broad is little Wood End Staithe for those who want to seek it out. A small mooring and grassy area provides a pleasant spot for a break, tucked away and rarely visited. It's also not that easy to find, so have fun looking. Home to the Norfolk Punt Club, the broad also hosts the Barton Broad Open Regatta across the Bank Holiday weekend at the end of August. Here, many different types of sailing craft compete in races around courses the length and breadth of the broad, so be aware this is a busy place if you are planning a trip around this time. There are plenty of places to explore, and both the fishing and wildlife watching opportunities are excellent.

Leaving the broad at the southern end via the

stretch of water known as 'The Shoals' due to its shallow, gravelly bed, you come to the little village of Irstead. If you are planning to stop off at Irstead, perhaps for a picnic or to see their picturesque thatched church and houses, be sure to only use the Broads Authority (BA) moorings and not the parish staithe next to it. The BA section is well marked while the other part of the staithe is for the use of parishoners only. If you are going to launch here, please look to the path leading to the BA staithe to the left of the car park as you look at the river and not the parish one directly in front of the parking area.

Continuing on its path south past Irstead, the Ant then weaves through a mixture of marshland, trees and pasture, and comes to How Hill. As you approach How Hill from the north, you pass Clayrack Drainage Mill. One of only two 'hollow post' drainage mills left on the Broads, it was moved here in 1981 from 2.5 miles away as it could not be restored in its old location without disturbing the wildlife. Next to Clayrack Mill is Boardman's Mill and just beyond you will find the moorings for How

Ludham Bridge.

Hill. This is a popular stop-off point with excellent moorings, although these can be quite busy in the summer months.

Ludham Bridge (21) is only a short distance further on and has plenty of mooring space. Launching here is easy with good car parking along the roadside and an easy drop-in. Both wind and current can be fairly strong here, and you often find quite a few motor boats coming and going from the moorings through the narrow bridge arch, so have your wits about you. Shortly after Ludham Bridge the Ant joins the River Bure opposite the entrance to South Walsham Broad and close to the picturesque ruins of St Benet's Abbey. It

How Hill Estate

Unfortunately the house itself is not open to the public, but is used as a study centre. The 365 acre estate boasts beautiful gardens and some magnificent views over the local area. The Edwardian house was built in 1904 by a Norwich architect as a family holiday home and is one of the largest thatched houses in Norfolk. On the estate

you will find Toad Hole Cottage. Originally a home for marshmen and their families in Victorian times, it now houses a Broads Authority information centre and a museum to life working the marshes for thatching materials, game, agriculture and tending to the drainage mills. The cottage has seasonal opening times, so check before you go.

was here in 2010 that the remains of a Saxon boat were found during flood defence works. The oak dugout also contained five animal skulls and once restored will be on view at the Norwich Castle Museum.

River Thurne

The River Thurne covers an area from Hickling, with its associated broad, and Horsey Mere in the north-east of the area. Used as a base for seaplanes in World War I, Hickling Broad covers an area of 5.9 square kilometres and can present some very different challenges to the paddler used to having calm waters and riverbanks either side of them. In times of strong winds, the waves can be fairly large and the broad gives a good sense of real open water to anyone who has only previously been on small rivers or canals. A sail on your canoe or kayak can be useful and greatly adds to the fun.

Hickling is the largest of the broads and you can easily spend a day paddling around it exploring inlets and reedy islands. The Pleasure Boat Inn at **Hickling Staithe (22)** has good quality food and drink with parking and easy launching for canoes and kayaks.

Horsey Mere is a wildfowl haven and paddling is not permitted between 1st November and 1st March. However, when access is allowed, Horsey Mere is a great place to paddle and the channel that connects the mere with Hickling Broad is well worth exploring. The only broad to be called a mere, the name comes from the fact that it is surrounded by a high-level bank. The word mere means artificial lake in old Dutch. Launching of canoes and kayaks is allowed from **Horsey Mill (24)** directly onto the mere, although there may be a small fee payable. The car park is owned by the National Trust and is not expensive.

The Pleasure Boat Inn, Hickling Staithe.

📷 *Hickling Broad 24-hour mooring.*

As you paddle out onto Horsey Mere you can spend a little time exploring. Head north, or simply keep to the right bank as you pass the little thatched cottage, and you find the entrance to Waxham New Cut. After around two kilometres of fairly narrow water it passes the now derelict, but still impressive, Brograve Drainage Mill, originally built in 1771. Connecting Horsey Mere with Hickling Broad is Meadow Dyke. The entry to Meadow Dyke is not that easy to see from across the mere, but if you head opposite to where you have just come out of the channel from the mill you should find it. It is really easy to find when a sailing boat is coming down the channel as you will see their mast and sails acting like a flag for you. Meadow Dyke is only about 10 metres wide for most of its length, and passing other boats along this narrow channel takes patience and some friendly communication with the captains. Keep to the right-hand side of the channel and don't be tempted to cut corners. There's not much room to manoeuvre and some of the motorboats come round the bends quite quickly, so beware. If you do pass

a slow-moving sailboat, do it quickly because the boat may have to tack as it rounds a bend. After around half a kilometre you will see the entrance to Stubbs Mill Dyke. This narrow channel is perfect for paddlers with the adventurous spirit as it really makes you feel like an explorer. Leading to the disused Stubbs Mill it provides a respite from other craft, very welcome if you are paddling this stretch during high season.

If you paddle this route in high summer or early autumn you will marvel at the sheer numbers of dragonflies and damselflies that are all around you. Often they will fly alongside you only an arm's length away as they hunt. In the autumn months particularly you will see mating pairs buzzing around frantically as they search for reed stems on which to lay their eggs just below the water surface. Hickling Broad is a refuge for the rare Norfolk hawker dragonfly which is best seen in June or early July, and if you are lucky you have a good chance of seeing the beautiful swallowtail butterfly as well. The whole area is perfect for those of us who love our wildlife and regular sightings of the impressive marsh and hen harriers are common. These majestic birds can be seen swooping along just above the reeds and often will be very close to you as you paddle through. Indeed, sometimes your first sighting of them will be as they come over the reeds to the side of the river and fly over your head! With a wingspan of over a metre, that's a fairly impressive sight. Birdwatchers are spoilt for choice in this area with such delights as hobby, merlin, bearded tit, common crane and even the bittern all regular visitors here, although you are more likely to hear the bittern's booming call than actually see one.

As you exit Meadow Dyke, keep right and you will enter Deep-Go Dyke. This can be busier still with craft as they head to and from Hickling Broad and towards the Thurne River. Entering Hickling Broad itself and seeing the water really opening out before you, keep right and you should soon see a little round building that appears to be set back from the water's edge. This observation tower is mainly for bird watching and, as it has its own little landing stage, paddlers can work their way through the short channel and go up into it for a different perspective on where they are paddling. There are some very useful information boards in the hide, and chatting to

walkers and bird watchers that may be there is a great way of taking a break.

Once you are ready to resume the paddle across Hickling Broad or start craving that refreshment at the Pleasure Boat Inn, head back out of the hide channel and turn right towards the middle of the broad. The posts that mark out the channel for the larger craft provide a useful path to follow. Keep to the right of the channel but beware as you approach the middle of the broad where you see some smaller, yellow posts sticking out of the water. This marks some very shallow water and there are a couple of submerged posts here, so keep clear and don't try to paddle straight through.

If you look to your left as you pass this point you should see some smaller red and green buoys over towards the far side of the broad. This is the entry to **Catfield Dyke (23)** and

[📷] Hickling Broad.

[📷] Hide mooring.

leads up a delightful but short channel to the public staithe. There is an alternative launching point at this staithe, but it is small and even if only three boats are moored up, paddlers cannot get in or out. It is well worth exploring though as it is picturesque, peaceful and a great place to spot kingfishers.

Back on Hickling Broad, if you continue on your original course towards the Pleasure Boat Inn, you should soon see a large grouping of masts and a couple of houseboats in the distance. If you aim for just to the left of the houseboats you will see the entry to the short dyke that leads to the pub. Just at this point there is also a small beach on your left, don't land here as it is privately owned by the boat club. Paddle up close to the pub and enjoy your respite before paddling on.

The River Thurne itself flows from **West Somerton (25)** in the east and winds its reed-lined way west through Martham Broad and then Martham Ferry with its chain bridge.

📷 *Martham Ferry Chain Bridge.*

There used to be a fixed bridge here but it was replaced by the floating swing bridge in the 1920s. The area of land to the north of the river is Heigham Holmes nature reserve which can only be accessed via the swing bridge, and even then only between the start of April and the end of October. Check the National Trust website for details if you are planning a visit. This is the alleged site of a secret WWII airfield that was used for ferrying allied agents into occupied Europe. Unfortunately no evidence of the airfield or

📷 *Catfield Dyke.*

📷 *Potter Heigham Bridge.*

📷 *Ludham Staithe.*

its buildings exists today. For kayak anglers, this area is well-known for its large pike, especially through the winter months. Martham Boats have excellent facilities for car parking and launching of boats close to the village of **Martham (26)** itself and this is a great place to start from if you are looking for a longer paddle exploring Hickling Broad and its surrounding waterways. Interestingly, the name Martham in the old Saxon tongue means 'the home of the polecats'. Presumably this relates to there being a high population of martens at the time and not just a criticism of the local Saxons.

Next the Thurne passes the popular village of Potter Heigham and under the famous medieval bridge believed to date from 1385. This is well-known as the most difficult bridge on the Broads to pass under, and pausing here in high season to watch the hire boats struggling with the low bridge and fast current can be rather fun; just beware of other craft as you traverse the bridge arches. Launching is possible right next to **Potter Heigham Bridge (27)** from Phoenix boat hire who will happily let you put in, especially for a contribution

towards their coffee and biscuits fund. There is also pay and display car parking close by as well.

Around a mile downstream from the bridge you pass the launching point at **Repps with Bastwick (28)** which is also the access to Willowcroft Campsite. Only a short distance from the water, this campsite has become popular with paddlers looking to explore the area.

A little further downstream you reach the entry to Womack Water which in turn leads to **Ludham Staithe (29)**. Womack Water is extremely picturesque, but the staithe is usually busy with cruisers mooring stern on to the bank so launching and landing here can be difficult at peak times of the year.

Thurne Dyke (30) and village itself is only a little further on. It welcomes paddlers with the impressive white windmill known locally as Morse's Mill, and together with the Lion Inn it makes a good point for a break. Launching here is possible and the Lion Inn is a great place to visit. Shortly afterwards the Thurne joins with the River Bure.

River Wensum (Norwich City)

The city of Norwich has seen many centuries of human activity. It has grown from several early settlements clustered around the river, through the Roman and Saxon periods, and later became an extremely busy and affluent medieval town. This growth has not always been smooth and the city has had its ups and downs. Norwich had great prosperity and wealth for much of the medieval period, but also had the dubious honour of being the only city ever excommunicated by the Pope, following a riot in 1274.

Norwich's colourful history has always been intrinsically linked with the River Wensum, and while it formed a vital part of the city's defences it also provided a means of attack. In the year 1004, the city was raided and burned by a fleet of Viking ships under the control of the wonderfully-named Swein Forkbeard, while the civil uprisings and rebellion under Kett in 1549 saw even more destruction.

The river is a great way to see the city, and a paddle through Norwich gives a unique view of the city that relatively few ever experience. As you travel through the city, picture the ever-changing riverside bridges and buildings ranging from wooden huts and houses to factories and mills, while fleets of ships and smaller boats transport everything from grain to wool, stone for the imposing cathedral or even smuggled booze destined for one of the riverside taverns. Telltale signs and remnants of this turbulent past are all around you as you casually cruise by.

The Wensum enters the Broads area close to the heart of Norwich at **New Mills (31)**. The mill was rebuilt in 1897 into the building we now see, but there has been a mill on this site for many hundreds of years. Launching here is fairly easy via the steps on the far side of the mill and it is a great place to start exploring the river. Paddling this particular stretch of the Wensum is very different from the rural

Norwich from the River Wensum. Photo | istockphoto.com

[📷] Swan pit.

type of paddling that most of us enjoy. Paddling through this area at night can be a fantastic experience, although this should not be attempted by either novice or solo paddlers.

Heading downstream from New Mills you first pass under the green, cast iron Coslany Bridge. Built in 1804 it replaced an earlier 16th-century bridge, although there has been a bridge here since at least the 12th century, and this was one of several river crossing points used to enter the city in Saxon times. Next is the bridge at Dukes Street which is also known as the Dukes Palace Bridge since the home of the Duke of Norfolk was nearby during the 16th century. The bridge here is a replacement for the 19th-century cast iron bridge which can now be seen as part of the entrance to the Castle Mall car park in the city centre. Just beyond this bridge, nestling amongst trees on the left, you will see the little brick building of the Norwich Playhouse Theatre whose patron is Stephen Fry.

Passing under the next bridge and rounding the bend you pass the slipway at Friars Quay and head under Fye Bridge. This is thought to be the oldest part of the city and evidence of Saxon and even Viking occupation has been found in the area. It is certainly known to be the oldest crossing point into the city. Interestingly, a plaque on the current bridge indicates that this was the location for a 'ducking stool' used to punish 'strumpets and common scolds'. It was also used for judging whether an accused woman was a witch or not. If she drowned she was innocent, if she survived she was judged a witch and burned. Not a great outlook either way for the woman concerned.

The next bridge you pass under is Whitefriars, named after a local order of 13th-century Carmelite monks. Religion has played a significant role in Norwich's history. In the Middle Ages 57 churches could be found within the city walls, and the spires and towers of many of the 31 that still exist today can be seen from the river. Indeed, there was even a saying that Norwich had a church for every week of the year and a pub for every day.

On the left, as you come to the next bend in the river and pass under an organic-looking footbridge, are the old offices for the Broads Authority before they relocated. Almost immediately after, and quite tricky to find on the southern bank, is possibly the only remaining 'swan pit' left in England. From the medieval period onwards, pits or enclosures were dug and filled with water to house cygnets. These birds would have their wings clipped to stop them flying away and were fattened up ready for the table. Picture that Sunday roast. Shortly after the pit, as you approach the next sharp right-hand bend you will see the imposing structure that is the Cow Tower. A very rare building of its type, this free-standing artillery tower was built at the end of the 14th century and dominates this strategically important location as part of the city defences. It is called the Cow Tower as it sits on an old water meadow that used to be known as Cowholme. It was reputedly damaged during Robert Kett's rebellion in 1549 by cannon fire from Mousehold Heath, prior to them storming the gatehouse on Bishop Bridge and gaining entry to the city. There is a little beach just after the bend on the right where you can stop and have a break or visit the tower.

Bishop Bridge is the next bridge you pass under and is the oldest bridge crossing the Wensum into Norwich. Built around 1340 the bridge was originally fortified with an imposing gatehouse and it controlled access

[📷] Cow Tower. Photo | istockphoto.com

to the western side of the city. Situated by the bridge is **The Red Lion (32)** pub. A great place to pause for refreshments and the owners will allow paddlers to park on their premises and launch. Just remember to ask first and promise to be back for a very satisfying respite afterwards. A couple of minutes

[📷] Bishop Bridge and The Red Lion pub.

THE RIVERS AND THEIR ASSOCIATED BROADS

downstream from the bridge is Pull's Ferry and the Cathedral Watergate. Pull's Ferry is named after John Pull the ferryman who carried people across the river here during part of the 19th century. The beautiful Cathedral Watergate was built in the 15th century and gave access to a small canal, cut originally in the 12th century, which was used to transport stone brought in from Normandy to build the cathedral. Construction of the cathedral itself began in 1096, shortly after Norwich Castle began to be built, and was finished in 1145.

Next you pass under Foundry Bridge, so named because of the foundry that used to stand here in the 19th century, just downstream of what is now the Nelson Hotel. Opposite the hotel you pass the *Lord Nelson*, a training ship for the Norwich Sea Scouts. Originally called the HMS *Vale*, a Swedish naval patrol boat, she was purchased by the Norwich Sea Scouts in 2003 at a cost of £30,000, and with a further refurbishment costing £93,000 and a change of name she is now a fitting headquarters for cadets to learn on.

Continuing through the popular Riverside area with its many pubs, restaurants and clubs, you pass under first the Lady Julian and then Novi Sad Friendship Bridges. Lady Julian of Norwich was a well-known local mystic born in 1342, and during a severe illness at the age of 30 when she believed she was on her deathbed, she experienced a series of intense visions of Christ. These ceased by the time she recovered but they formed the basis of her writings for which she is famous – the first book written in the English language by

TS Lord Nelson.

a woman. She eventually went on to live to the ripe old age of 73! Pretty impressive for the 15th century. Both footbridges are relative newcomers to the Wensum, being opened in 2009 and 2001 respectively to give better access to the Riverside area as it developed.

As you approach the final road bridge you will see Carrow Road football ground, home of Norwich City football club who are also known as the Canaries. So called due to the city once being a famous centre for the breeding and export of the birds. On a match day you will certainly hear it before you see it. Just the other side of the road bridge you pass the ruins of the round, stone Boom Towers. Built in the 14th century and part of the city wall defences, they controlled river access into the city, and originally had great chains of Spanish iron slung between them that could be raised or lowered by means of a windlass contained in one of the towers.

Just beyond Carrow Road you pass under the rail bridge at Trowse which connects Norwich Station to Ipswich, Cambridge and beyond. After the rail bridge you pass Carrow Yacht Club and the confluence with the River Yare, joining the Wensum from the right.

River Yare

Shortly after the confluence with the Wensum, the Yare passes Whitlingham Country Park and Broad with its Outdoor Education Centre, the home of Norwich Canoe Club and where many people take their first guided steps into the world of paddlesports. A large floating pontoon gives superb access onto the river here, although if you are thinking of launching here, the walk from the car park is fairly lengthy and a trolley to carry your boat would be advisable. Alternatively you can park at the visitor centre a little further down the road with a car park closer to the broad.

Thorpe Green can be reached by taking the left fork under the railway bridge shortly after the pontoon at Whitlingham Broad and along this little loop of water you can stop off at any one of a number of riverside pubs for a break. Just at the start of the loop is **Cary's Meadow (33)** launch point, situated opposite the offices of Broadland Council which makes finding this spot extremely easy. This newly-established portage point which gives access from the north side of the river is a fantastic development for paddlers who live in the city.

Keeping straight on, or alternatively paddling under the railway bridge and through the loop at **Thorpe St Andrew (34),** takes you around past **Whitlingham Broad (35)** and another newly-developed launching point. This can be found at the bottom of Whitlingham Lane where there is now access to the river by the **Whitlingham Woods car park (36)**. This provides ample car parking, a short, easy portage to the river and a safe launching point. Please use the car park, as parking on the road may result in a parking fine.

Continuing downstream from here the river gradually works its way east passing a few boatyards and then under the A47. Just beyond

☐ *River Yare and River Waveney. Photo | Mark Rainsley.*

is the outflow for the sewage works on the southern bank so be aware that there may be a slight odour along this stretch at times.

It doesn't take long for the A47 traffic noise to die away and the river is now framed by mature woodland and then farmland that weaves towards the Water's Edge pub. This used to be The Woods End pub but has now been completely renovated with a great riverside seating area. There is a slipway here but parking is an issue for launching. A little further on from the Water's Edge is the mooring at **Bramerton Common (37)**. Stopping here can be a little tricky as it is often busy with cruisers and there are only a couple of ladders to enable you to get out onto the bank. Launching is possible here as there is car parking, but again the vertical drop-in and ladders may put some paddlers off.

Beyond here the scenery opens out and this is a beautiful, winding stretch of river that brings you to the next potential stopping place. The Ferry House pub has one of the, if not *the*, most friendly of welcomes on the Broads. A newly-installed slipway here will make this little watering hole a perfect starting, stopping and pausing place for paddlers. A great menu and variety of drinks make The Ferry House a worthwhile waypoint. Opposite is **Postwick Wharf (38)**, a great place to launch from as this is one of the very few launching points on this part of the Yare that is accessed from the northern side of the river.

The Yare now returns to wooded banks and gentle bends and shortly after The Ferry House you pass a couple of boatyards, and then on the southern bank you will find the first entrance that gives access to picturesque Bargate and Surlingham Broad. This small broad is popular with boaters looking to anchor up and enjoy some lazy summer sun, but it also has some smaller waterways that the bigger boats can't get down but paddlers certainly can, and this is well worth a break to go wild and explore. Look for the sign stating 'shallow water' and a little inlet with a good flow. Paddle up here and there is another world to explore; narrow, winding waterways that merge and split with very few landmarks to guide you back – just don't get lost! Reeds and Himalayan balsam tower over you obscuring the horizon and muffling sounds giving you a real sense of exploration. It's a great feeling paddling though this wilder environment and do keep an eye out for otters!

Returning to the broad you can either paddle back out onto the river the way you came or continue straight through and out via the second entrance opposite Brundall Marina and very close to the Coldham Hall pub. An immaculately-presented waterside pub with a little beach area that is ideal for canoes and kayaks to pull up onto, Coldham Hall is a very welcoming place for a break.

A little further on and the river passes the entry to Rockland Broad, again on the southern bank. This broad is worth exploring as it not somewhere that the cruisers generally go. It is a great place for watching wildlife or just paddling about peacefully and with ample parking close to the water, **Rockland Broad (39)** is ideal for beginners looking to gain a little confidence. Parking here is free with easy launching and the broad has plenty of inlets and islands to explore. Indeed some of the islands on the western side of the broad are actually the wrecks of old wherries that have become overgrown. You might see wrecks emerging from the waters of many of the broads, as during WWII the military commandeered boats and dotted them around the larger broads in an attempt to prevent enemy seaplanes landing as part of an invading task force. These hulls now form islands, parts of the banks, and occasionally mid-water obstructions which you will see marked with yellow poles to warn boats of their presence. From Rockland paddling downstream, you may see the white clouds emanating from the chimneys of the sugar beet processing plant

which tell you Cantley is not far away. This was the first sugar beet processing factory in the UK, originally built in 1912. The Yare continues on for some distance passing the Beauchamp Arms pub and Langley Dike (a short but very pleasant distraction and very different from the current river, with stunning mature trees on both sides, which leads to **Langley Staithe (40)** launch point) and then the excellent staithe and easy launching for paddlers at **Cantley Staithe (41)** with the Red House pub only a couple of kilometres further on.

This part of the river and beyond is not travelled by paddlers very often as it is sometimes described as fairly bland scenery, and it can be busy with cruisers and affected by strong tidal forces. Nonetheless, with careful planning and an understanding of the tidal forces at play, this can still be a rewarding and enjoyable paddle.

📷 *Beauchamp Arms.*

Langley Dyke.

even built a lighthouse here as a navigation aid for their ships as they traversed the water around the Yarmouth area.

After Reedham the river splits and heads either north-east past the Berney Arms pub towards Burgh Castle and Great Yarmouth, or south-east through New Cut to join the River Waveney heading towards Oulton Broad and Lowestoft. The Berney Arms, another location mentioned in the *Swallows and Amazons* book *Coot Club* can only be accessed by foot, train or boat, and sits almost on the confluence of the Yare and Waveney rivers at the southern-most end of Breydon Water. For anyone looking to paddle on across Breydon Water and onto the Bure, this is a good place to stop and rest ready for that challenge. Breydon Water can be extremely difficult and unpredictable to cross. In windy conditions 2–3 feet high waves are not uncommon and a very large tidal range means that careful planning is essential. As you pass under the road bridge at the northern end of Breydon Water, look for the large yellow post that marks the entrance to the Bure.

Continuing along the reed-lined Yare here, you pass the confluence with the Chet on the southern bank at Hardley Cross. The Chet is a short stretch of water which takes you along a wonderful, picturesque, winding river passing Hardley Flood and on to the village of Loddon. It only takes around an hour each way and is well worth exploring. Just after the meeting point of these two rivers, you come to the Reedham Ferry with its pub and touring park. Camping is available here and both the Ferry Inn and touring park are owned by the same people and the warmest of welcomes is assured. Just be aware that the chain ferry operates here carrying cars across the river. As you paddle this stretch of river, look around you at the horizons and see how wide the river basin is here. **Reedham (42)** formed part of the coastline two millennia ago, and the Romans

Reedham.

River Chet

A tributary of the River Yare, the Chet is only 5.5km in length and access for paddling is either in the village of Loddon, or from the Yare. Although not the longest of paddles, it can be a very pleasant trip as it winds its way passing Hardley Flood Nature Reserve and is lined with tall reedbeds and trees that are a haven for wildlife. Launching at **Loddon Staithe (43)** car park is fairly straightforward and your first two hours parking is free. Alternatively you can launch at **Pyes Mill (44)** on the other side of the village. If launching from the staithe, drop in by the footbridge, but beware there are some pieces of old wooden revetment just visible above the water that could cause problems if you're not ready for them when launching or landing. This first section of water has a very slow flow and is a very easy paddle as you pass houses and moorings and the Pyes Mill launch and picnic spot about 0.5km away. After around 15 minutes paddling, you start to pass Hardley Flood nature reserve on your left. Along here you come across a footbridge on your left where the water from the reserve drains out into the Chet at times of high water levels. This flow can be fairly strong and create some surprising eddies at this point, so be ready for it. Don't try to paddle up this water to get into Hardley Flood, the reserve is not open to paddlers and there are parts of the old wooden pilings that are exposed and could catch unwary paddlers out. The flow of the Chet increases from this point which makes paddling the return journey back towards

River Chet.

Ready to launch at Loddon Staithe.

Loddon that little bit harder. The rest of the Chet out towards the Yare is a series of tight bends and short straight sections. Be aware that both sides of the Chet have some very old wooden pilings that in places are in a less than perfect state of repair. There are signs all along the river banks warning of this, so beware of exposed metalwork if you get close to the banks or are thinking of stopping for a break.

The Chet joins with the Yare at Hardley Cross, a monument erected in 1676 which marks an old boundary between the city of Norwich and Great Yarmouth. Nearby is Reedham Ferry, and the pub there is a very nice place to stop before making the return journey.

River Waveney

The Waveney is a superb stretch of water that is great to paddle by kayak and is even better in a canoe. Technically the river enters the Broads area at Geldeston Lock, but there is an access agreement in place allowing paddlers to enjoy much more and it would be a crime not to include it in this guidebook. Starting at Harleston, with a launch point by **Shotford Bridge (45)** on the B1123, sets the scene for the kind of paddling you are going to encounter as you wind your way through the beautiful Waveney Valley. Frequently challenging to the paddler, with sharp bends, thick weed, varying depths and fallen trees a regular feature, the Waveney is a highly rewarding river to explore. The foundations of the old Shotford Bridge can be seen at the launch point, and when the old bridge was demolished in the 1950s, a large WWII land mine was discovered and removed by the Bomb Disposal Squad. All the munitions for the nearby Metfield airbase were transported over the bridge and presumably the land mine was placed in case the strategically important bridge needed to be destroyed in case of invasion.

The river weaves its way through floodplains and grazing pastures under Mendham Bridge towards the portage point at Mendham Mill. The mills along this part of the Waveney are in private hands and the grounds are people's gardens, so please be respectful and considerate as you portage around them. Built in 1820 the mill has been beautifully restored and, along with the cottages on the site, offers luxurious accommodation. At Mendham Mill the river forks and the portage is via the north bank, left as you paddle downstream. Around another 2km further on is the second portage at Wortwell Mill, also known as Limbourne Mill. A mill has stood on this site since the time of the Domesday Book. Once again portage on the north bank (left). If you launch back into the small stream, be aware that there are sluices here that can be potentially hazardous. For less experienced paddlers it is advisable to portage a little further and launch once you are clear of the sluices.

◎ Looking across the River Waveney.

◎ Mendham.

Homersfield Sluice lies only a short distance further on and this is another obstacle where portaging is advised. Take the left fork and portage via the south bank on your right; re-launch close to the large tree. **Homersfield Bridge (46)** is a welcome sight. It is the oldest concrete bridge in Great Britain and was built in 1870. Just after the bridge are the egress points for the picnic area on your left and the Black Swan pub to your right, where paddlers have always been assured a warm welcome. Camping is even granted to paddlers by prior agreement with the management, and calling in advance is requested.

Homersfield Bridge plaque.

From the Black Swan the river weaves through open pasture and thick woodland as it approaches the next portage at Earsham Mill. This mill dates back to the Saxon period and the portage is via the southern bank on your right and past the sluice. Once past the sluice take the right-hand fork. The final stretch towards Bungay finds you once again paddling through pasture with another potential launch point at **Bungay Castle (47)** next to the

Bungay Castle.

ivy-covered, castle-style walls on your right. Continuing under the beautiful footbridge and past the houses you pass under the road bridge and enter what has become known as the 'Bungay Loop', a short stretch of water that circles the town and which can be quite busy with paddlers in the summer months.

The River Waveney forms the boundary between Norfolk and Suffolk and works its leisurely way from Bungay through some idyllic scenery past Geldeston and Beccles towards Oulton Broad and finally Lowestoft. With a much smaller amount of boat traffic and the limit of navigation to motorised craft at Geldeston Lock, the upper reaches of the Waveney around Bungay present the paddler with some truly beautiful water to explore. The most southerly launching point, and indeed the first launching point on the Waveney within the Broads area, is **Outney Meadow (48)** campsite just to the west of Bungay. The campsite here has been run by the same family for many years and is a wonderful place from which to start exploring the Broads. The campsite is well set up to accommodate

📷 *Outney Meadow.*

📷 *Outney Meadow.*

paddlers, with excellent launching facilities and a fleet of canoes for hire. Launching here you can either paddle upstream around the Bungay Loop or downstream past Bungay and onwards towards Ellingham and Beccles.

The Loop section of the river is an ideal place to start; slow-moving, beautifully clear water with some wonderful views across the meadows to welcome paddlers. Indeed, if you are new to canoes and kayaks and looking for a first paddle, this is ideal and will only leave you wanting more. This stretch is also perfect for families, and taking a picnic is practically a must. Stopping along the bank is permitted and there are plenty of places to get out for a break and some refreshment, but please remember to stay close to the river as further from the water it is private land. Even though the scenery is the thing most people notice, there are still some points of interest to take note of.

As you paddle upstream, after around two kilometres you will see a beautiful, white cottage on the north bank. This is Bath House, once the home of Lilias Rider Haggard, daughter of Henry Rider Haggard who created the

character Allan Quatermain. Indeed, the writer of such novels as *King Solomon's Mines* lived in Ditchingham, just to the north of Bungay and is buried in the local St Mary's Church.

If you choose to paddle downstream from Outney Meadow you quickly come to your first portage point. Portages on this stretch of the Waveney are excellent, with superb quality areas designed specifically for paddlers to pull up and get out. The walk here around **Bungay Sluice (49)** is only short and the path is very well maintained. Alternatively, there is a small, free car park here at the River Centre so you can also use this as a starting point,

📷 *Bungay Sluice.*

although the car park can be a little tricky to find first time around. This is also the home of the Waveney Canoe Club, so best behaviour! It is just under a kilometre paddle to the next portage point at **Wainford Bridge (50)** through the beautiful Waveney Valley open countryside and, like at Bungay, the portage points are well signposted and maintained. The sluice is also cordoned off with a floating barrier, so simply look to the right and you will see where to get out. Simply drop back in on the other side of the sluice and then paddle under the bridge.

More stunning views over the lush Waveney Valley await the paddler onwards from here through to **Ellingham Sluice (51)** and sadly, this is currently where the last easy portage greets you. Across the road getting back onto

the water presents more of a challenge. The water here is partly governed by the Bungay Cherry Tree Angling Club and discussions over access for paddlers were ongoing for many years. Happily though, there is now an agreement in place and work on improving the launching here is currently under way to install a dedicated portage point. To access the river on the downstream side, look for the stile a few metres south of the gate on the opposite side of the road, and then keeping to the footpath head back towards the river.

This next stretch is one of the most beautiful on the Broads. The wildlife is abundant and the paddling experience is superb. The river from here is affected by the tides and water levels can vary. Paddlers need to be aware of possible bottoming out and trying to minimise any

📷 *Wainford Bridge.*

Ellingham Bridge portage west.

disturbance of the riverbed. Around every bend you are greeted by abundant, friendly wildlife, and the kind of glorious picture opportunities that can turn any of us from casual, happy snappers into budding wildlife photographers. Having a camera with you on this stretch really is a must, but remember to have it in a water-proof pouch as accidents do happen.

Slowly the river meanders through the countryside sheltered by trees as it winds its way lazily towards **The Locks Inn at Geldeston (52)**. As you pass under the bridge just before the pub, be aware that this is the mooring for the ferry and from here onwards you may well start to encounter motorboats. The Locks Inn was originally a 16th-century lock keepers cottage and it was granted its first licence in the 17th century. The pub is a regular stopping point for canoeists and kayakers arriving from either Beccles or Bungay. The welcome is warm and friendly, the food is excellent and the local ales are superb. A huge garden area with tables is available, but most of the time you can simply sit on the grass close to the water. If you want to start your trip from here, park in the first large car park area you come to as you drive down the unmade road towards the pub. It is only a short walk from here to the pub and river. **Rowan Craft (53)** is also in Geldeston; this business allows paddlers to park and launch from their slipway for a small fee and is also a member of the Broads Hire Association with a small fleet of canoes for hire. They also have pitches for caravans making it ideal for cara-vanners who also paddle.

From Geldeston the Waveney travels towards Beccles through more idyllic canoeing territory. On approaching Beccles, you see the town up

Locks Inn, Geldeston.

Rowan Craft.

Beccles quay and slipway.

on the hill to the right and soon reach the busy area at **Beccles Quay (54)** just before the road bridge. There are often motor craft manoeuvring here so a little caution is advised. There is a free slipway here, so stopping for a break is very easy. The handy close-by car park is free for the first 2 hours and then a small fee by the hour or for all day makes this an ideal starting point.

Once under the road bridge the river remains calm and easily paddled, with gently winding stretches lined with mature alder to the left. All along this part of the river a footpath follows along the right bank, so you'll often have company as you cruise by. Around two miles from Beccles you will begin to see the remains of the East Suffolk Line railway swing bridge that used to cross the river here until the 1960s. Only the large brick-built footings remain but they give a good impression of just how large the bridge would have been.

From this point on the riverbanks change from leafy trees to more reed-lined, and the wildlife changes also. Dragonflies become more evident, and whereas birds such as the willow warbler, chiffchaff and if you are lucky, and at the right time of year, perhaps even a cuckoo can be heard along the earlier stretch, through the reeds you are far more likely to be serenaded by reed warbler and bunting, while large birds of prey wheel above you riding the thermals. The impressive grey heron is also a fairly common sight along the river banks as you paddle by.

You soon come to the **Waveney River Centre (55)** which with its camping area is an ideal place to use as an overnight stay if you are on a longer expedition, or even as a starting point or just as a lunch break. Not far from here you reach the confluence of the Waveney and Oulton Dyke channel joining from the south which leads to the broad itself. Oulton is a fairly large broad with many beautiful properties and the imposing 19th-century maltings buildings. Power boat racing is occasionally held on the broad, you'll certainly hear it before you see it, but be aware that if the racing is on there will only be certain parts of the broad you can access. All the events are advertised in advance and very well marshalled so there

Waveney River Centre pike.

is little danger to paddlers. Paddling around Oulton Broad is a very pleasant experience, its wide expanse of water is bordered by some very nice properties and makes for a great paddling venue. There is a convenient slipway with ample parking and for beginners it is a good place to gain on-the-water experience. Heading north from Oulton Dyke the river is once more framed by reedbeds and distant horizons as you approach first **Somerleyton Staithe (57)** and then the junction of the Waveney with New Cut. This perfectly straight stretch of water acts like a short cut to Reedham and the River Yare whereas continuing on the right fork brings you to St Olaves Bridge. **The Bell Inn at St Olaves (58)** is a really nice pub and the owners are happy for paddlers to drop in or even launch from their moorings; just make sure to ask inside first. The food is also very good, so if you are paddling this stretch keep it in mind for a lunch break.

Oulton Dyke confluence sign.

The final section of the Waveney is quite long and takes you past the Roman fort of Burgh Castle before meeting the River Yare and finally opening out onto Breydon Water. The current can gradually get stronger closer to Breydon Water, Great Yarmouth and the entrance to the River Bure, with ever increasing tidal forces at play, so if you are planning to paddle around this area, make sure you have appropriate safety equipment, plan your trip carefully, and be aware of the tide times and weather.

River Waveney from Beccles.

Table of Launching Points

Map no.	River	Location	Postcode	Grid ref	Parking / waypoint	Portage to water (metres
1	Bure	Horstead Mill	NR12 7AT	TG266193	Free	25/120
2	Bure	Belaugh Staithe	NR12 8XA	TG288185	Free	10
3	Bure	Hoveton Riverside Park	NR12 8UR	TG302183	Free	50
4	Bure	Wroxham Broad	NR12 8TS	TG307166	P&D	10
5	Bure	Salhouse Broad	NR13 6RX	TG319150	Donation	700
6	Bure	Horning	NR12 8AA	TG340175	P&D	40
7	Bure	Woodbastwick Staithe	NR13 6HN	TG343164	Free	10
8	Bure	Malthouse Broad	NR13 6AB	TG359145	Free	80
9	Bure	South Walsham Broad	NR13 6ED	TG372139	Free	75
10	Bure	Upton Dyke	NR13 6BL	TG402127	Free	25
11	Bure	Stokesby	NR29 3EX	TG430105	Free	10
12	Ant	Honing Lock	NR28 9PJ	TG331270	Free	20
13	Ant	Dilham Staithe	NR28 9PS	TG332255	Free	20
14	Ant	Wayford Bridge	NR12 9LL	TG347248	Free	35
15	Ant	Smallburgh Staithe	NR12 9LL	TG347247	Free	35
16	Ant	Stalham Staithe	NR12 9DA	TG372247	Free	20
17	Ant	Sutton Staithe	NR12 9QS	TG382237	Free	35
18	Ant	Barton Turf	NR12 8AZ	TG357224	Free	25
19	Ant	Neatishead Staithe	NR12 8BJ	TG344209	Free	30
20	Ant	Gay's Staithe	NR12 8XP	TG350209	Free	200
21	Ant	Ludham Bridge	NR29 5NX	TG371170	Free	30 – 100
22	Thurne	Hickling Staithe	NR12 0YW	TG409225	Charge	50 – 100
23	Thurne	Catfield Dyke	NR29 5BP	TG400212	Free	100
24	Thurne	Horsey Mill	NR29 4EF	TG456222	P&D	50
25	Thurne	West Somerton	NR29 4AB	TG467199	Free	150
26	Thurne	Martham	NR29 4RF	TG438191	P&D	50

Launching permitted	Vertical drop-in	Available slipway	Picnic facilities	Toilets	Notes
Y	Y	Y	Y	N	Norfolk's only whitewater
Y	Y	Y	Y	N	
Y	Y	N	Y	N	First four hours free
Y	Y	Y	Y	N	
Y	Y	Y	Y	Y	Donation for launching. Slipway actually a beach
Y	Y	Y	N	N	Launch from staithe
Y	Y	Y	Y	N	Risk of access road flooding. Slipway actually a beach. Camping also vailable
Y	Y	N	Y	Y	Very busy peak season
Y	Y	Y	N	N	
Y	Y	Y	Y	N	
Y	Y	N	Y	N	Last public access before Great Yarmouth
Y	Y	N	N	N	Very narrow channel to launch into – not lock
Y	Y	N	N	N	Parking very limited to roadside
Y	Y	Y	N	In pub	Patronise Wayford Bridge Inn
Y	Y	Y	N	N	Small launching fee. 12 foot max length
Y	Y	N	N	N	Launch from Stalham Staithe
Y	Y	Y	N	N	Charge avoided if launch from BA 24-hour mooring
Y	Y	N	N	N	Sign states 'no launching' – applies to groups
Y	Y	N	N	N	Use ladders at end of staithe
Y	Y	N	N	N	Park in BA car park
Y	Y	N	N	Y	Launch on southern side of bridge (downstream)
Y	Y	N	Y	Y	Enquire at Pleasure Boat Inn
Y	Y	N	N	N	Launch from public staithe only. Track to walk down first
Y	Y	N	Y	Y	Launching fee payable if bailiff present
Y	Y	N	N	N	Do not launch from parish staithe
Y	Y	Y	N	Y	Launch from boatyard – small charge (additional to parking)

TABLE OF LAUNCHING POINTS

Map no.	River	Location	Postcode	Grid ref	Parking / waypoint	Portage to water (metres)
27	Thurne	Potter Heigham Bridge	NR29 5JQ	TG420184	P&D	75
28	Thurne	Repps with Bastwick	NR29 5JU	TG413174	Free	10
29	Thurne	Ludham Staithe	NR29 5QG	TG391180	Free	10
30	Thurne	Thurne Dyke	NR29 3AP	TG403158	Pub	40
31	Wensum	New Mills	NR3 3AH	TG226090	Various	250
32	Wensum	Red Lion	NR1 4AA	TG239090	Y	10
33	Yare	Cary's Meadow	NR7 0DU	TG252084	Free	200
34	Yare	Thorpe St Andrew	NR7 0EW	TG260083	Free	30
35	Yare	Whitlingham Broad	NR14 8TR	TG250078	P&D	350
36	Yare	Whitlingham Woods Car Park	NR14 8TS	TG269078	P&D	30
37	Yare	Bramerton Common	NR14 7ED	TG294060	Free	30
38	Yare	Postwick Wharf	NR13 5DU	TG307075	Free	10
39	Yare	Rockland Broad	NR14 7HP	TG327046	Free	50
40	Yare	Langley Staithe	NR14 6AD	TG365027	WP	25
41	Yare	Cantley Staithe	NR13 3SH	TG382034	Free	15
42	Yare	Reedham	NR13 3TE	TG419016	Free	10
43	Chet	Loddon Staithe	NR14 6EZ	TM361989	P&D	20
44	Chet	Pyes Mill	NR14 6DS	TM366990	Free	30
45	Waveney	Shotford Bridge (Harleston)	IP20 9QT	TM246822	Free	10
46	Waveney	Homersfield Bridge	IP20 0ET	TM283857	Free	20
47	Waveney	Bungay Castle	NR35 1DE	TM334897	Free	20
48	Waveney	Outney Meadow	NR35 1HG	TM333904	Fee	200
49	Waveney	Bungay Sluice	NR35 1BF	TM340897	Free	50
50	Waveney	Wainford Bridge	NR35 1TA	TM350901	Free	20
51	Waveney	Ellingham Sluice	NR35 2EX	TM364916	Free	20
52	Waveney	Geldeston (The Locks Inn)	NR34 0HS	TM389908	Free	100
53	Waveney	Geldeston (Rowan Craft Ltd)	NR34 0LY	TM389917	Free	50
54	Waveney	Beccles Quay	NR34 9BH	TM423911	P&D	50
55	Waveney	Waveney River Centre	NR34 0BT	TM492934	Fee	100
56	Waveney	Oulton Broad	NR33 9JR	TM518924	P&D	100
57	Waveney	Somerleyton Staithe	NR32 5QR	TM475970	Free	10
58	Waveney	St Olaves (The Bell Inn)	NR31 9HE	TM458994	Free	25

Launching permitted	Vertical drop-in	Available slipway	Picnic facilities	Toilets	Notes
Y	Y	Y	Y	Y	Launch at Phoenix Boat Hire - charge
Y	Y	N	N	N	Access to Willowcroft Campsite
Y	Y	N	Y	Y	Very busy peak season
Y	N	Y	N	Y	Ask in pub for parking
Y	Y	N	N	N	Steps down to water
Y	Y	N	N	Y	Check with pub for details
Y	Y	N	N	N	
Y	Y	Y	Y	N	
Y	Y	N	N	N	Excellent launching facility
Y	Y	N	Y	N	
Y	Y	N	Y	N	Can be busy and tricky launch in peak season
Y	Y	Y	N	N	
Y	Y	Y	Y	N	Donation for slip use
Y	Y	N	N	N	BA 24-hour mooring
Y	Y	Y	Y	N	
Y	Y	N	Y	N	
Y	Y	N	Y	Y	Launch by footbridge
Y	Y	N	Y	N	Height restriction
Y	Y	N	N	N	Car park height restriction
Y	Y	N	Y	N	Height restriction
Y	Y	N	N	N	
Y	Y	N	N	Y	
Y	Y	N	N	N	Car park open between 07.00 and 22.00
Y	Y	N	N	N	
Y	Y	N	N	N	
Y	Y	N	N	Y	Paddlers should patronise pub
Y	N	Y	N	Y	Access via Rowan Craft 01508 518208
Y	N	Y	N	Y	First 2 hours free
Y	Y	Y	N	Y	
Y	N	Y	N	N	
Y	Y	N	Y	N	BA 24-hour mooring
Y	Y	N	N	N	BA 24-hour mooring

Catfield Staithe, River Thurne.

· Catfield Staithe ·

Free Moorings

Maximum stay 24 hours

Launching Point Descriptions by River

River Bure

1 Horstead Mill

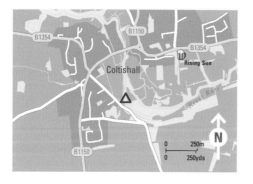

Horstead Mill Sluice.

OS Explorer OL40 Grid Ref: TG 266 193
Postcode: NR12 7AT

This marks the starting point for the Broads Authority area of the River Bure.

Launching at Horstead Mill presents the paddler with two choices. Those wanting a more adventurous start can walk from the car park to the side of the mill pond where the ground slopes gently to the flowing water's edge. It can be quite a challenge getting in or out of your boat here as the bank can also be quite muddy. However, this is an excellent spot to have a little fun in the faster stuff, and is just about Norfolk's only whitewater experience.

Note: The slipway is for parishioners' use only. Alternatively, if you walk over the mill sluices from the car park and turn left you can launch into the still waters by the lock where there is also a slipway to help you enter the water gracefully.

📷 *Bure at Horstead.*

Upstream of Horstead Mill is free water and as such no Broads Authority permit is required. This stretch of the river, while not covered as a part of this guide, is extremely beautiful and would be a shame to miss out. So if you are planning a trip from or around the Coltishall area, the upper part of the Bure from Horstead Mill is highly recommended.

Directions

From Norwich – take the B1150 towards Coltishall. On entering Horstead village, continue down the hill until just before the roundabout with the Recruiting Sergeant pub opposite, turn right down Mill Road and the entrance to the mill car park is around 300 metres on your left.
From Wroxham/Hoveton – take the B1354 into Coltishall. At the junction with the petrol station on your right, turn left onto the B1150 towards Norwich. Immediately after the roundabout which has the Recruiting Sergeant on your right, turn left down Mill Road. After about 300 metres turn left into the car park for the mill.
From Great Yarmouth – take the A47 towards Norwich until you reach the Blofield and Brundall roundabout. Here, you need to turn back on yourself, heading back along the A47 but only for just over half a mile. You will soon see a signpost for Blofield Heath and shortly after a filter lane for this exit. Follow the signs through Blofield Heath and out the other side of the village until you come to a junction. Turn left here and after just under a mile you will come to a crossroads with The Brick Kilns pub on your right. Turn right here onto Honeycombe Road and stay on this road following the signs for Wroxham. After you drive over Wroxham Bridge and past Roys department store you come to the first of a pair of small roundabouts. Turning left here puts you onto the B1354 towards Coltishall and simply follow the instructions above from Wroxham/Hoveton.

2 Belaugh Staithe

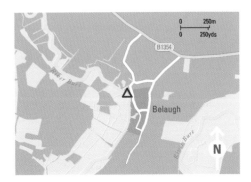

OS Explorer OL40 Grid Ref: TG 288 185
Postcode: NR12 8XA

The tiny village of Belaugh can be a little tricky to find. If you do manage to discover it there is a potential launching spot here onto the River

Bure. The parking is free but very limited with space only for about four vehicles. Launching is via a vertical drop of about a metre, but certainly still manageable for both canoes and kayaks. The Broad Authority has improved this facility and there is now a great slipway to the water's edge right next to the car park. Picnic tables, benches and a well-kept grassy area also make it a very pleasant place for a short break or a picnic as it lies about halfway between Horstead Mill and Wroxham.

Directions

Belaugh lies between the villages of Coltishall and Hoveton just off the B1354. The access road and signpost to the village are fairly small, so don't blink or you'll miss it.

From Norwich – take the A1151 into Wroxham and after you drive over Wroxham Bridge and past Roys department store you come to the first of a pair of small roundabouts. Turning left here puts you onto the B1354 towards Coltishall and Belaugh. Continue under the Bure Valley Railway bridge and onwards for about half a mile. Take the next left onto Top Road signposted for Belaugh. It has dead-end signs, but don't let that put you off. A little way on, turn right onto The Street and follow this road round where suddenly you will find yourself at the riverside car park area.

From Wroxham/Hoveton – take the B1354 towards Coltishall and follow the directions as above.

From Great Yarmouth – take the A47 towards Norwich until you reach the Blofield and Brundall roundabout. Here you need to turn back on yourself, heading back along the A47, but only for just over half a mile. You will soon see a signpost for Blofield Heath and shortly after a filter lane for this exit. Follow the signs through Blofield Heath and out the other side of the village until you come to a junction. Turn left here and after just under a mile you will come to a crossroads with The Brick Kilns pub. Turn right here onto Honeycombe Road and stay on this road all the way following the signs for Wroxham. After you drive over Wroxham Bridge and past Roys department store you come to the first of a pair of small roundabouts. Turning left here puts you onto the B1354 towards Coltishall and then you simply follow the instructions as above.

Paddler at Belaugh.

3 Hoveton Riverside Park

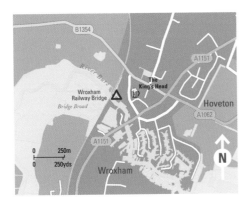

OS Explorer OL40 Grid Ref: TG 302 183

Postcode: NR12 8UR

It is truly remarkable to find such a tranquil launching spot in the heart of the busiest village on the Norfolk Broads. This is the very centre of the boating industry for the area and most people would not even consider launching here, but it really could not be more simple. The ample car parking is close to the launch point, and as you walk towards the water you are greeted by a large decking area which helps to make launching and recovery easy.

Hoveton Riverside launching.

Overhanging willow trees surround you as you put in at this little backwater before paddling out under the arched footbridge and out onto the river. Turning left takes you towards Salhouse Broad, Horning and the larger broads at Malthouse and South Walsham, whereas turning right will lead you upstream to Belaugh, Coltishall and Horstead Mill.

Using this location as a waypoint is also a great idea as it is ideal for a picnic with good, well-kept grassy areas and benches. Just prepare yourself to be hassled by the ducks.

Directions

From Norwich – take the A1151 into Wroxham. After you drive over Wroxham Bridge, take the first left onto Station Road before you pass Roys department store. Follow this road and soon on the left you will see a signpost for Roys long stay car park, turn in and head for the far left corner of the car park which is close to the water. Parking here is free for up to four hours. If you are looking to stay and paddle for longer it may be better to use the launch site at Wroxham Broad, which is only 10 minutes away.

From Great Yarmouth – take the A47 towards Norwich until you reach the Blofield and Brundall roundabout. Here you need to turn back on yourself, heading back along the A47, but only for just over half a mile. You will soon see a signpost for Blofield Heath and shortly after a filter lane for this exit. Follow the signs through Blofield Heath and out the other side of the village until you come to a junction. Turn left here and after just under a mile you will come to a crossroads with The Brick Kilns pub. Turn right here onto Honeycombe Road and stay on this road all the way following the signs for Wroxham. Then simply follow the directions as above.

Wroxham.

4 Wroxham Broad

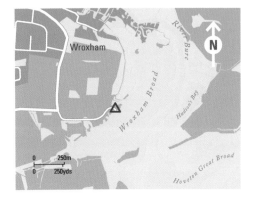

OS Explorer OL40 Grid Ref: TG 307 166

Postcode: NR12 8TS

A very good launching place, especially if you have an open canoe and a family. Wroxham Broad has a long waterside grassy area and a gently shelving sandy slipway. The vertical drop here is only around 30cm so putting in boats is very easy. The broad itself is large and gives good access to the Bure. Be aware that the members of the yacht club are regularly found sailing the broad in fairly large numbers; giving them a wide berth is a good idea. Once out onto the river, paddling upstream takes you to Wroxham and beyond towards Coltishall and Horstead Mill. Downstream is the

popular village of Horning and further along is access to the Rivers Ant and Thurne as well as some of the other larger broads. A pleasant short trip downstream from here is Salhouse Broad with its beach, grassy picnic area and small playground facility. This is only around a kilometre paddle, and as such is a great, short first trip for a family or someone trying out a new boat. This is probably the busiest stretch of river in the broads during the summer, so care needs to be taken when paddling.

Car parking at Wroxham Broad is pay and display but there is plenty of room and fees are very reasonable.

Coltishall Common.

Directions

From Wroxham/Hoveton – take the A1151 out of Wroxham towards Norwich and at the roundabout take the first exit onto the B1140. Then turn left onto The Avenue. A short distance on this road will bring you to a sharp left-hand bend with a gravelly road joining from the right. There is a sign opposite for the Norfolk Broads Yacht Club stating 'Public Pay and Display Car Park at End'. Head down this road and the car park is easily found just before the yacht club.

From Norwich – take the A1151 out of Norwich towards Wroxham. As you approach Wroxham and head over the railway bridge, you reach a small roundabout. Turn right here onto the B1140 and follow the instructions as above.

From Great Yarmouth – take the A47 towards Norwich until you reach the Blofield and Brundall roundabout. Here you need to turn back on yourself, heading back along the A47, but only for just over half a mile. You will soon see a signpost for Blofield Heath and shortly after a filter lane for this exit. Follow the signs through Blofield Heath and out the other side of the village until you come to a junction. Turn left here and after just under a mile you will come to a crossroads with The Brick Kilns pub. Turn right here onto Honeycombe Road and stay on this road all the way following the signs for Wroxham. After driving through Salhouse and passing The Bell Inn, you pass signs for The Lodge Country House on your right and then traverse a couple of small hills (yes, we have hills in Norfolk). Shortly after

the second hill is a right turn signposted for Wroxham Broad. Turn right here onto The Avenue and follow the directions as above.

---

5 Salhouse Broad

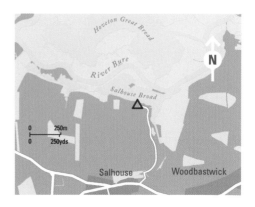

OS Explorer OL40 Grid Ref: TG 319 150

Postcode: NR13 6RX

Launching from Salhouse Broad involves a fairly lengthy walk from the car park along a mixture of pathways and boardwalk. For those who do make the trek, Salhouse Broad offers a great place from which to launch with a small beach and calm waters that are

Salhouse Broad Beach.

ideal for beginners. A trolley is almost an essential, and as you walk along be aware that this area is very popular with dog walkers so please watch where you're walking. Nothing scuppers a pleasant day in your boat more than an unwelcome smell from something a four-legged friend left behind. Alternatively, canoes and kayaks can be hired from here and overnight camping is even available. There is also a good play area for kids large and small. For more details contact the Ranger at Salhouse Broad directly on 01603 722775 or visit www.salhousebroad.org.uk where you can email them directly.

Directions

From Wroxham/Hoveton – take the A1151 out of Wroxham towards Norwich and at the roundabout take the first exit onto the B1140. Then turn left onto The Avenue. A short distance on this road will bring you to a sharp left-hand bend with a gravelly road joining from the right. There is a sign opposite for the Norfolk Broads Yacht Club stating 'Public Pay and Display Car Park at End'. Head down this road and the car park is just before the yacht club.

From Wroxham/Hoveton – take the A1151 out of Hoveton towards Norwich and at the first roundabout take the first exit (B1140) to Salhouse. Follow this road around the sharp right-hand bend and take the third left turn onto Vicarage Road signposted The Lodge Country House pub. Continue along this road through the village of Salhouse itself as it becomes Upper Street and finally you come

to a junction with a phone booth and small red post box to your right. Turn left here and the entrance to the car park for Salhouse Broad is around 400 metres away on your left.

From Norwich or Great Yarmouth – take the A47 to the Blofield Junction. Follow the signs for Blofield Heath and Woodbastwick. Stay on this road going straight over the junctions until you enter the village of Woodbastwick. Turn left onto Salhouse Road and past the Fur and Feathers pub and home of the Woodfordes Brewery. The entrance to the car par is around half a mile further on your right.

6 Horning

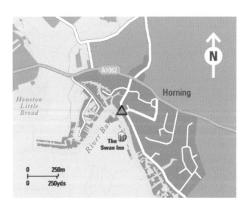

OS Explorer OL40 Grid Ref: TG 340 175
Postcode: NR12 8AA

Horning is one of the most popular destinations for people coming to the Broads. Parking is close to the water and launching is fairly easy with a small vertical drop-in. It is a beautiful village with some excellent riverfront pubs and restaurants in which you can while

📷 *Horning Ferry Staithe parking.*

Horning. Approximately half a mile after passing the Bewilderwood Adventure Park on your left, you turn right onto Lower Road. The signpost here is towards Horning but just beyond you will see a sign with red writing on for RRH Neatishead. If you pass this red sign, you've gone too far! There is a small pay & display car park a short distance down Lower Road close to The Swan Inn. However, if you continue past The Swan you will see Mill Loke road on your left; turn right here into a small car park for the staithe. Parking here is free but limited to two hours. If you are planning to stay for longer, or the car park is busy, you can park for free at the village hall just across the road.

From Great Yarmouth – follow the A47 towards Acle. At the Acle roundabout take the third exit (A1064). After around two miles take a left turn onto the B1152 signposted for Martham, North Walsham and The Broads. Follow this road until you reach a junction with the A149 and turn left following the signs for Cromer, North Walsham and The Broads. After around half a mile you will go over Potter Heigham Bridge where shortly after you turn left onto the A1062 signposted for Horning and Ludham. Follow the signs for Horning as you pass through the village of Ludham and then over Ludham Bridge. Resist the urge to turn left at the first signpost for Horning Lower Street, but rather continue on until you see a large signpost with RRH Neatishead in red. This is pointing right and immediately after this you will see the left turn for Horning and follow the directions as above.

away the summer afternoons and evenings, enjoying good food and watching the world go by in its boat. This popularity can come at a price for the paddler in that the larger craft can make the area a little challenging in the busiest months. Saying that, it is nothing to be too worried about, but beginners may feel slightly intimidated with the number of craft on the water. Small shops, a café and also The Swan Inn are all close to the launch point for refreshments. If you are launching at the staithe you may see a sign stating that launching is limited to boats of 12 feet maximum. This does not apply to canoes and kayaks.

Directions

From Norwich, Wroxham/Hoveton – as you head north out of Hoveton on the A1150 you approach a set of double roundabouts. Take the A1062 (Horning Road) signposted towards

7 Woodbastwick Staithe

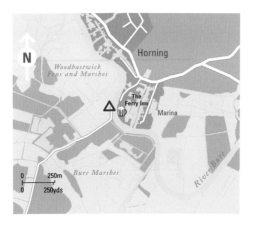

OS Explorer OL40 Grid Ref: TG 343 164

Postcode: NR13 6HN

On the opposite bank to Horning village itself, Woodbastwick Staithe, or the ferry launching point, represents an easy way to access this section of the River Bure in the busy summer months. It is away from the main tourist car parking area and the launching point rarely suffers from other boats being moored along its length. There is a shallow beach-like area at the end of the car park which is a perfect spot for launching.

There are a couple of potential drawbacks to this site, however. While car parking is free, it is a little limited, but more serious than this is that at times of high tides the river level can rise dramatically and flood the access road. Not too much of an issue for a 4x4 owner, but normal cars can struggle.

Paddling upstream from here takes you towards Salhouse Broad, Wroxham and Coltishall, while downstream are the broads of Malthouse and South Walsham and access to the Rivers Thurne and Ant.

Directions

From Wroxham/Hoveton – take the A1151 out of Hoveton towards Norwich and at the first roundabout take the first exit (B1140) to Salhouse. On entering the village there is a left turn following a sharp left-hand bend just by the Bell Inn. This is Salhouse Road and will take you into the village of Woodbastwick. On entering the village you will see Woodforde's Brewery and pub on your left, and if you continue on this road you will pass through the village and later the Fur and Feathers pub (home of the Woodforde's Brewery) and the church. After the next sharp left-hand bend you approach a sharp right-hand bend and road heading off straight ahead with signs stating that the road is liable to flooding. Turn left here onto Ferry Road and continue to the car parking and launch point. Be aware that this section of road is liable to flood at times of high tides so check the water levels before you go!

From Norwich or Great Yarmouth – take the A47 to the Blofield junction. Follow the signs for Blofield Heath and Woodbastwick. Stay on this road going straight over the junctions until you enter the village of Woodbastwick. Turning right here and then onto Ferry Road as described above.

8 Malthouse Broad

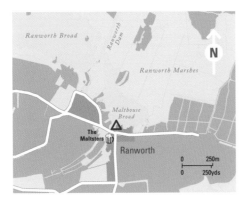

OS Explorer OL40 Grid Ref: TG 359 145

Postcode: NR13 6AB

Actually in the village of Ranworth, Malthouse Broad is a busy place with many motor cruisers mooring here in the summer months. Ranworth Broad is not accessible as it is a protected wildlife area. There is a small car park area close to the water and plenty of further free parking available opposite The Maltsters pub. Public conveniences are situated here as well. There is a tourist information office and shop should you require them, and launching is via a small vertical drop of less

📷 *Malthouse Broad.*

than 50cm just behind the building. A good-sized grassy area including picnic tables can also be found here, but this will be busy during the summer as coach parties are fairly common. Cruisers moor stern on here but they are not allowed into the launching area for paddlers so present little problem.

Once you are out onto the River Bure, upstream will take you towards Horning and Wroxham, while downstream are South Walsham Broad and entries to the Rivers Ant and Thurne.

Directions

From Wroxham/Hoveton – take the A1151 out of Hoveton towards Norwich and at the first roundabout take the first exit (B1140) to Salhouse. At the next roundabout take the first exit (B1140) towards Acle. After Panxworth, the B1140 splits off to the right, but keep heading straight on as this is now the Panxworth Road and will take you in the right direction. Just after South Walsham village take the Ranworth Road and this will lead you straight to the broad. Park in the car park opposite The Maltsters pub.

From Norwich/Great Yarmouth – take the A47 towards Acle and shortly after North Burlingham turn left onto the B1140 (South Walsham Road) signposted for South Walsham and Fairhaven Water Gardens. After just under two miles turn right at the signpost for South Walsham, then right again at the junction with The King's Arms on your left. After only 200 metres turn left onto Ranworth Road which takes you straight to the broad. Park in the car park opposite The Maltsters pub.

From Great Yarmouth – take the A47 towards Acle and then towards Norwich. After around 1.8 miles take the right turn onto the South Walsham Road (B1140) and follow the directions as above.

9 South Walsham Broad

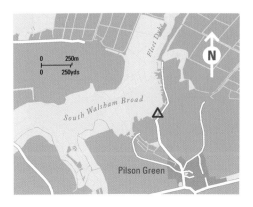

Explorer OL40 Grid Ref: TG 372 139
Postcode: NR13 6ED

South Walsham is one of the larger broads and indeed you could paddle around the extensive water here all day exploring its tree-lined borders, coves and inlets. Parking here is free with plenty of spaces and only a couple of hundred metres from the low vertical drop-in. There is a slipway here and the local parish is happy for recreational paddlers to use it for launching. Please be aware that they don't have to do this, but generously do so, please treat this with respect.

South Walsham Broad is a great starting point from which to explore the tree-lined section of the Bure and a good, short paddle trip is from here to Malthouse Broad and back. This is also probably the best starting point for those wanting to see St Benet's Abbey from the water and not have to paddle too far. Alternatively the broad itself is a pleasant location to spend a couple of hours paddling and exploring.

Directions

From Wroxham/Hoveton – take the A1151 out of Hoveton towards Norwich and at the first roundabout take the first exit (B1140) to Salhouse. At the next roundabout take the first exit (B1140) towards Acle. After Panxworth, the B1140 splits off to the right but keep heading straight on as this is now the Panxworth Road and will take you in the right direction. Just after about a third of a mile you come to a crossroads. Turn left here onto School Road following the sign for Fairhaven Water Gardens. You will soon come to a left turn sign posted simply 'Broad'. This is Broad Lane and the car park is around half a mile further on. It is situated on the left as you get to the Kingfisher Land road name sign. The launching point is 50 metres further on.

South Walsham Broad launching.

From Norwich/Great Yarmouth – take the A47 towards Acle and shortly after North Burlingham turn left onto the B1140 (South Walsham Road) signposted for South Walsham and Fairhaven Water Gardens. After just under two miles turn right at the signpost for South Walsham, then right again at the junction with The King's Arms pub on your left. Just after about a third of a mile you come to a crossroads. Turn left here onto School Road following the sign for Fairhaven Water Gardens and follow the directions as above.

From Great Yarmouth – take the A47 towards Acle and then towards Norwich. After 1.8 miles take turn right onto the South Walsham Road (B1140) and follow the directions as above.

10 Upton Dyke

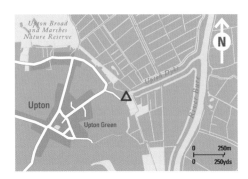

OS Explorer OL40 Grid Ref: TG 402 127

Postcode: NR13 6BL

Just north of Acle sits the small village of Upton. Ironically, despite its small size, Upton has probably one of the best and biggest free car parking and launching sites of anywhere

📷 *Upton Dyke launching.*

on the Broads. Although not easy to find first time around, it is a very good launching point for those looking to paddle longer trips along the Bure, Ant and Thurne. A slipway and picnic area make this a great starting point or simply a place to break up a paddle trip.

South of here the river can be affected by tides with strong currents, so the recreational paddler needs to be aware of this and take it into account when planning an outing.

Directions

From Wroxham/Hoveton – take the A1151 out of Hoveton towards Norwich and at the roundabout just after the petrol station take the first exit (B1140) towards Salhouse. Follow this road into Salhouse where at the next roundabout take the first exit onto Low Road (B1140) towards Acle. After Panxworth the B1140 splits off to the right, but keep heading straight on as this is now the Panxworth Road and will take you in the right direction. Continue through South Walsham and staying on this road you will come to a couple of fairly sharp right then left bends. Just over half a mile further on from these you will find a left turn signposted to

Upton. This is Church Road and leads into the village itself. Passing over the first crossroads you come to a right turn opposite the White Horse pub signposted to Boat Dyke. Take this turn and a little further on turn left onto Boat Dyke Road. Follow the road until you approach a dead-end sign. To the left you will see a couple of entries to the car parking area and a Broads Authority sign for Upton Dyke.

From Norwich/Great Yarmouth – take the A47 to Acle and head for the village centre. At the village centre simply follow the signs for Upton. These will lead you out of the village and through a little countryside until you reach a right turn still signposted for Upton. This is now Church Road and from here follow the directions as above.

📷 Upton Dyke car park.

Tidal information

By checking the tidal data for Gorleston and then the 'High Tides Around the Broads' spreadsheet you can work out when high tide will hit the area of the Broads you are paddling.

11 Stokesby

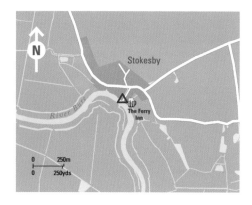

OS Explorer OL40 Grid Ref: TG 430 105
Postcode: NR29 3EX

Easy to find with free all day parking right by the river, a large grassy park featuring old-style playground equipment and a nice waterfront pub; these factors make Stokesby a great place for launching or just breaking up a journey. Families will appreciate the playground facilities and it is ideal for a picnic, although there are no tables and only a couple of benches, so bringing a rug with you is a good idea. The Ferry Inn serves good quality food and drink with a traditional pub menu at reasonable prices. The waterside seating area is perfect for watching the world go by as you recover after your paddle or refuel ready for the return trip. A vertical drop-in at the staithe of around 50cm makes launching easy; there is a slipway towards the pub, but this is privately owned and not to be used. Tidal range can affect the flow and water level here, so take that into account when planning your paddle.

📷 *Stokesby playground.*

Directions

From Wroxham/Hoveton – take the A1151 out of Hoveton towards Norwich and at the roundabout just after the petrol station, take the first exit (B1140) towards Salhouse. Follow this road into Salhouse where at the next roundabout take the first exit onto Low Road (B1140) towards Acle. After Panxworth, the B1140 splits off to the right and you will see it signposted for Great Yarmouth and Acle. Turn right here and continue until you reach the A47. Turn left onto the A47 and continue to the Acle roundabout. Take the second exit onto the A1064 signposted towards Caister-on-Sea and after just over a mile turn right onto New Road which is signposted for Stokesby. About mile down this road you enter the village and after passing a couple of old terraced cottages on your right which are right by the road, you immediately turn right. The car parking area is a few metres on and is right by the river.

From Norwich/Great Yarmouth – take the A47 to the Acle roundabout. At the roundabout take the A1064 signposted towards Caister-on-Sea and follow the directions as above.

River Ant

12 Honing Lock

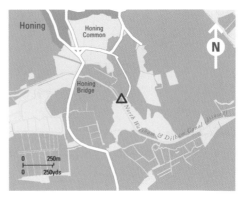

OS Explorer OL40 Grid Ref: TG 331 270

Postcode: NR28 9PJ

Honing Lock is the first available access point on the North Walsham and Dilham Canal to access The Broads area. A beautiful short stretch of water with a real wilderness feel, be aware that there may be weed or tree obstructions at points along this route. Though technically this is private water it is currently possible to paddle, please note a

📷 *Canoes on the Dilham Canal.*

donation box has been installed at Tonnage Bridge by the landowner who also owns the water. Access for paddlers is by his good grace but be aware that this could change at any time. The lock can be a little tricky to find...

Directions

From Norwich/Wroxham/Hoveton – take the A1151 towards Stalham, turning left onto the A149 signposted for Cromer, North Walsham and Smallburgh. After approximately a mile you come into Smallburgh; the road winds down into a dip and immediately after you see a right turn signposted for Dilham. The sign is on your left and quite small so keep a sharp look out. This road is simply called 'The Street', later becoming Honing Road, and will take you all the way into Honing. Follow this road until you come to the first brick-walled bridge and just after, a metal-walled bridge followed by left-hand bend. Just beyond the bend the road seems to almost split into three directions by the signpost for Honing. Take the right-hand fork here and then quickly right again. Through the woodland you take the next right turn just after the signpost for East Ruston, followed by right again only a few metres further on. This is Locks Road and will take you all the way to the parking area. As you drive past the houses you see fencing on either side of the road, as though there should be a gate barring the way, and a very small gravelly area on the right just beyond. Further past here is a sign stating 'Private' so please

stop here. The lock is only around 20 metres walk down the path.

From Great Yarmouth – take the A149 out of Great Yarmouth towards Stalham. Continue on the A149 through Stalham and over Wayford Bridge. Shortly after the garage on your right, take the next right signposted A149 for Cromer, North Walsham and Smallburgh and follow the instructions as above.

---

13 Dilham Staithe

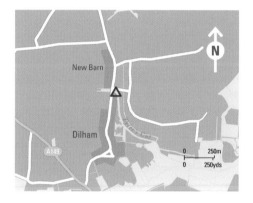

OS Explorer OL40 Grid Ref: TG 332 255
Postcode: NR28 9PS

Dilham Staithe allows you to explore all the overgrown inlets of this area of water towards Wayford Bridge. A long section of moorings with a small vertical drop-in and large grassy area makes it ideal for a break and a picnic if you are having a day out paddling from the bridge or further afield. The only issue with launching here is the lack of good parking. There are a couple of very small roadside spaces to pull into. There is also a fairly narrow (but certainly not difficult, even with an open canoe) gap at the end of the hedge to get through and access the staithe.

Directions

From Norwich/Wroxham/Hoveton – take the A1151 towards Stalham, turning left onto the A149 signposted for Cromer, North Walsham and Smallburgh. After approximately a mile you come into Smallburgh; the road winds down into a dip and immediately after you see a right turn signposted for Dilham. The sign is on your left and quite small so keep a sharp look out. This road is simply called 'The Street' and as you drive through Dilham the road bends round to the left flanked by houses. As you approach the staithe, the houses are only present on your right with a field on your left. At the end of these houses you will see the road narrows with brick-walled sides. Park around here and the entry to the staithe is on your right before these walls, between the hedge and last house.

From Great Yarmouth – take the A149 out of Great Yarmouth towards Stalham. Continue on the A149 through Stalham and over Wayford Bridge. Shortly after the garage on your right, take the next right signposted A149 for Cromer, North Walsham and Smallburgh and follow the instructions as above.

14 Wayford Bridge
(The Wayford Bridge Inn)

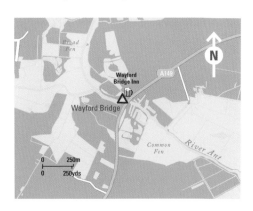

OS Explorer OL40 Grid Ref: TG 347 248
Postcode: NR12 9LL

Launching is possible here with permission from the Wayford Bridge Inn. Simply drop in and check with the landlord first, have a paddle and then come back for some of their fine fare. If the inn is too busy then Smallburgh Staithe is only the other side of the bridge.

Directions

From Norwich/Wroxham/Hoveton – take the A1151 from Norwich through Wroxham towards Stalham. After passing through Smallburgh you pass a petrol station on your left and then a bridge over the river where you will see the Wayford Bridge Inn on the far bank. Take the left turning into their car park just after the bridge.

From Great Yarmouth – leave Great Yarmouth on the A149 and follow the signs for Potter Heigham and Cromer. Drive over Potter Heigham Bridge and continue through

Stalham where you will pass a Tesco supermarket on your right. As you continue out of Stalham pass the Meale and Sons farm shop and then the Wayford Bridge Inn is on your right just before the bridge over the river.

15 Smallburgh Staithe

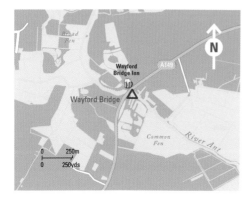

OS Explorer OL40 Grid Ref: TG 347 247

Postcode: NR12 9LL

Launching at Smallburgh Staithe is restricted to canoes and kayaks of 12 foot and under. There is a small donation of £3 requested for launching and is payable to Bank Boats just to the right of the slipway. Car parking close to the slipway is free and there is room for around ten cars.

From the staithe turn left and under the bridge to head up the Dilham Canal towards Honing Lock, or right to paddle down the Ant towards Barton Broad and Ludham Bridge. The confluence with the Yare lies a short distance beyond Ludham with St Benet's Abbey an interesting stopping point.

Directions

From Norwich/Wroxham/Hoveton – take the A1151 from Norwich through Wroxham towards Stalham. After passing through Smallburgh you pass a petrol station on your left and then see a sign stating 'Boat Hire' pointing right. Take the next right turn almost immediately after the sign and follow this round for about 150 metres. Car parking is by the staithe.

From Great Yarmouth – leave Great Yarmouth on the A149 and follow the signs for Potter Heigham and Cromer. Drive over Potter Heigham Bridge and continue through Stalham where you will pass a Tesco supermarket on your right. As you continue out of Stalham pass the Meale and Sons farm shop and then the Wayford Bridge Inn on your right. Just after the sign indicating you are entering Smallburgh a road joins from the left. Turn left here and follow this round for about 150 metres. Car parking is by the staithe.

Smallburgh Staithe.

16 Stalham Staithe

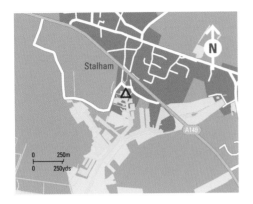

OS Explorer OL40 Grid Ref: TG 372 247

Postcode: NR12 9DA

The parking at Stalham Staithe is roadside only, and while it is a quiet back road it can be a little off-putting. Portage to the waterside is around 10 metres and the drop-in is easy, simple and small enough to manage with both canoes and kayaks. Stalham Staithe is a very pleasant location and great starting point for a longer paddle through the boatyards and out to Barton Broad. The Museum of the Broads is also located here.

Directions

From Norwich/Wroxham/Hoveton – take the A1151 from Norwich through Wroxham towards Stalham. After you pass under the average speed cameras you will see a Tesco supermarket on your left. Around a third of a mile further on there is a centre lane for turning right onto Staithe Road. Turn right here and the car park for the staithe is around 350 metres further along on your left.

From Great Yarmouth – leave Great Yarmouth on the A149 and follow the signs for Potter Heigham and Cromer. After you drive over Potter Heigham Bridge you soon come to a crossroads with the Sutton Staithe Hotel on your left. Just under a mile further on you are entering Stalham and come to a large metal barn-style building on your left with a road junction. Turn left here onto Staithe Road and the car parking is along the road by the staithe.

17 Sutton Staithe

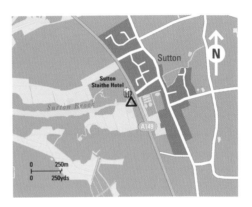

OS Explorer OL40 Grid Ref: TG 382 237

Postcode: NR12 9QS

Sutton Staithe is a good place to launch in the summertime due to the small inlet that only paddlers can realistically use. As you enter the ample Sutton Staithe car park you can either park in the first area or try your luck past the hotel and by the bins. There is only space here for a couple of cars, but it does save you the walk from the car park if there is room, and the drop-in is right there next to it. Otherwise you can simply launch over the side of the staithe closest to the car park which is only around 30 metres from the car park.

Similar to Stalham Staithe, Sutton is a good starting point for longer paddle trips down to Barton Broad and beyond. It can be a little less busy in the summer and easier to access Barton Broad without having to go through the boatyards at Stalham.

Directions

From Norwich/Wroxham/Hoveton – take the A1151 from Norwich through Wroxham towards Stalham. After you pass under the average speed cameras you will see a Tesco supermarket on your left. Around a third of a mile further on from here you pass a large metal barn-style building as you leave Stalham. Around a mile further on you come to a crossroads with the right turn signposted for Sutton Staithe and signs for the hotel also here. Turn right and the car park is on your left.

From Great Yarmouth – leave Great Yarmouth

📷 *Sutton Staithe.*

on the A149 and follow the signs for Potter Heigham and Cromer. After you drive over Potter Heigham Bridge you soon come to a crossroads with the Sutton Staithe Hotel on your left. Turn left here and the car parking for the staithe is on your left.

---

18 Barton Turf

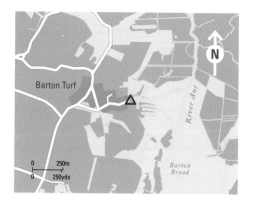

OS Explorer OL40 Grid Ref: TG 357 224

Postcode: NR12 8AZ

There are many options for day trips around Barton Broad, the River Ant and North Walsham & Dilham Canal, and Barton Turf is the ideal starting point for this area. Free parking, although this can be a little limited during the busy summer months, and a small vertical drop-in make launching and landing easy. The large sign that states 'No launching' relates to groups rather than individuals or families. Be aware that this can be a busy location with other craft coming and going to the moorings, so take care when paddling out between the boats.

Directions

From Norwich/Wroxham/Hoveton – take the A1151 from Norwich through Wroxham, Stalham and Cromer. Shortly after you have passed through Hoveton on the A1151 you come to a right turn signposted towards Barton Turf and Neatishead. Turn right here and follow this road into and through Neatishead village. Just after the village centre and sharp left-hand bend by the White Horse pub you come to a right turn signposted for Barton Turf. Turn right here onto Hall Road and continue towards the village. You soon come to the large Barton Turf sign by the pond. Turn right here and the staithe is only a short distance further on.

From Great Yarmouth – leave Great Yarmouth on the A149 and follow the signs for Potter Heigham and Cromer. Drive over Potter Heigham Bridge and continue through Stalham passing a Tesco supermarket and later the Meale and Sons farm shop and then the Wayford Bridge Inn on your right. Continue over the bridge and you will pass a petrol station and then the turning for the A149 towards Cromer on the right. A little further on you come to a crossroads with the left turn signposted towards Neatishead and Barton Turf. Turn left here and then next left again onto Mill Road which is signposted for Barton Turf. Just as you pass the 'Reduce Speed Now 30 zone' signs, turn right. Turn left at the next junction and you should see the large Barton Turf sign by the pond. Turn right here and the staithe is only a short distance further on.

19 Neatishead Staithe

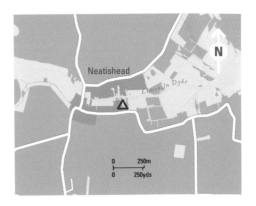

OS Explorer OL40 Grid Ref: TG 344 209

Postcode: NR12 8BJ

This is a good place to launch and access Barton Broad but can be very busy in the summer months with moored-up cruisers and cars in the car park. The car park at Neatishead is only small with parking for about eight cars. However, if there is space to park and the staithe looks full, you should still be able to launch at the far end of either side of the staithe. The vertical drop-in reduces to around only 30cm at the far end of the staithe and there is a ladder at both sides for easy access/egress.

Directions

From Norwich/Wroxham/Hoveton – take the A1151 from Norwich through Wroxham, Stalham and Cromer. Shortly after you have passed through Hoveton on the A1151 you come to a right turn signposted towards Barton Turf and Neatishead. Turn right here and follow this road into and through Neatishead village. At the village centre and on the sharp left-hand bend by the White Horse pub, turn right onto Irstead Road. Passing houses on your left you soon come to the left turn into the car parking area for the staithe.

From Great Yarmouth – leave Great Yarmouth on the A149 and follow the signs for Potter Heigham and Cromer. Drive over Potter Heigham Bridge and continue through Stalham passing a Tesco supermarket and later the Meale and Sons farm shop and then the Wayford Bridge Inn on your right. Continue over the bridge and you will pass a petrol station and then the turning for the A149 towards Cromer on the right. A little further on you come to a crossroads with the left turn signposted towards Neatishead and Barton Turf. Turn left here and follow the road into Neatishead village. Shortly after entering the village you come to a sharp right-hand bend with a road joining from the left opposite the White Horse pub. Turn left here onto Irstead Road and follow the directions as above.

⬚ Neatishead Staithe.

20 Gay's Staithe

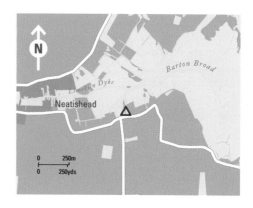

OS Explorer OL40 Grid Ref: TG 350 209
Postcode: NR12 8XP

Gay's Staithe is often a handy second option for launching if Neatishead Staithe is busy with a lot of hire cruisers moored up and the car park full. You park in the Broads Authority car park for Barton Broad Boardwalk and the access track to Gay's Staithe is only a short walk away. The launch point can be busy with cruisers, but as you reach the end of the track immediately to your left you will see a ladder dropping to the water level. This is probably the easiest place to get in if it is busy and the vertical drop is only around 50cm.

Directions

From Norwich/Wroxham/Hoveton – take the A1151 from Norwich through Wroxham, Stalham and Cromer. Shortly after you have passed through Hoveton on the A1151 you come to a right turn signposted towards Barton Turf and Neatishead. Turn right here and follow this road into and through Neatishead village. At the

📷 *Gay's Staithe.*

village centre and on the sharp left-hand bend by the White Horse pub, turn right onto Irstead Road. Follow this road past Neatishead Staithe and take the next right turn. As you approach the national speed limit signs you should see the entrance on your left into the car park for Barton Broad Boardwalk. Park here and walk back along the road, turn right at the junction and the entry to the path accessing the staithe is around 30 metres further on the left.

From Great Yarmouth – leave Great Yarmouth on the A149 and follow the signs for Potter Heigham and Cromer. Drive over Potter Heigham Bridge and continue through Stalham passing a Tesco supermarket and later the Meale and Sons farm shop and then the Wayford Bridge Inn on your right. Continue over the bridge and past a petrol station and a right turning for the A149 towards Cromer. A little further on you come to a crossroads with the left turn signposted towards Neatishead and Barton Turf. Turn left here and follow the road into Neatishead Village. After entering the village you come to a sharp right-hand bend with a road joining from the left opposite the White Horse pub. Turn left here onto Irstead Road and follow the directions as above.

21 Ludham Bridge

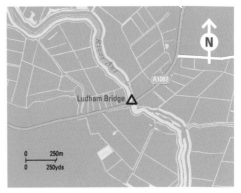

OS Explorer OL40 Grid Ref: TG 371 170

Postcode: NR29 5NX

Ludham Bridge is a good place to launch, but do be careful when loading boats or portaging to and from the water as the road can be busy during the summer. The easiest place to launch is on the right-hand side of the bridge as you walk from the roadside parking, as the drop is slightly less than on the left, however there are lengthy moorings to the left. The current here can be fairly fast through the arch depending upon the tides, and as the bridge sits on a bend in the river it can be quite

📷 *Ludham Bridge.*

difficult to see oncoming motor craft. You will sometimes find cruisers performing 180 degree turns here, so watch out for them as they may not see you. This spot is also very popular with anglers, so be considerate when launching and landing, and talk to them if you will be paddling close to where they are sitting.

Directions

From Norwich/Wroxham/Hoveton – as you head north out of Hoveton on the A1150 you approach a set of double roundabouts. Take the A1062 (Horning Road) signposted towards Horning. Continue on this road past the village of Horning and you will come to a fairly straight stretch of road which approaches Ludham Bridge itself with lay-by style parking on the right-hand side. Park here and walk to the launching point either side of the bridge.

From Great Yarmouth – follow the A47 towards Acle. At the Acle roundabout take the third exit (A1064). After around two miles take a left turn onto the B1152 signposted for Martham, North Walsham and The Broads. Follow this road until you reach a junction with the A149 and turn left following the signs for Cromer, North Walsham and The Broads. After around half a mile you will go over Potter Heigham Bridge where shortly after you turn left onto the A1062 signposted for Horning and Ludham. Follow the signs for Horning as you pass through the village of Ludham and then over Ludham Bridge. Parking is alongside of the road on the left just the other side of the bridge.

River Thurne

22 Hickling Staithe

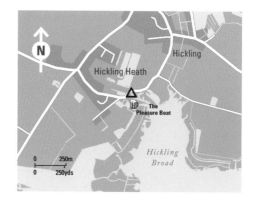

OS Explorer OL40 Grid Ref: TG 409 225
Postcode: NR12 0YW

Ample car parking close to the water makes this a good launching place for Hickling Broad. Beware of parking in the areas along the road as these are for parishioners only and you are likely to have an angry local on your back pretty fast. There is a charge for using the car park here, enquire at the Pleasure Boat Inn and they will charge you a small amount to launch. This is however redeemable on any later purchase of food or drinks and after paddling the broad you'll probably be glad of the refreshment. Portage to the water is only around 75 metres and launching is a vertical drop-in of about 75cm along the staithe by the pub. Avoid landing and launching from the beach at the end of the moorings as this is privately owned. Toilets are available at the end of the car park, or in the pub if you are stopping for refreshment.

TEL: 01692 598870

NO LAUNCHING OF CANOES
OR WINDSURFERS PLEASE

DINGHY (£6) & CANOE LAUNCHING (£4) AT PARISH STAITHE
INCLUDING PARKING SPACE . TICKETS CAN BE
PURCHASED AT PLEASURE BOAT INN BAR FROM 11AM

FOR WINDSURFERS TO GET ACCESS TO THE BROAD, JOIN
HICKLING WINDSURFING CLUB
Email: memberships@hicklingbroad.co.uk

Hickling Staithe parking.

Directions

From Norwich/Wroxham – as you head north out of Hoveton on the A1150 you approach a set of double roundabouts. Take the A1062 (Horning Road) and follow the signs for Horning, Ludham and then finally Great Yarmouth until you reach the junction with the A149 to either Stalham or Great Yarmouth. Turn left here towards Stalham and around a mile further on you come to a staggered crossroads with the road off to the right signposted for Hickling and Hickling Broad. Turn right here onto Potter Heigham Road and follow it into the village where first you pass a road on your left signposted towards Stalham opposite a red post box, and then a little further on you come to another staggered crossroad with the left turn towards Sutton and Stalham and then a right turn to Hickling Broad. Turn right here onto Staithe Road and follow the road until you come to a right turn into the car park for the Pleasure Boat Inn.

From Great Yarmouth – leave Great Yarmouth on the A149 and follow the signs for Potter Heigham and Cromer. Drive over Potter Heigham Bridge and past the turning left towards Ludham and Horning, and about a mile further on you reach the staggered crossroads as detailed above.

23 Catfield Dyke

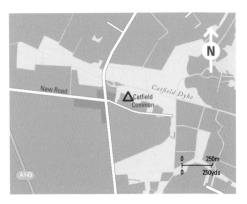

OS Explorer OL40 Grid Ref: TG 400 212
Postcode: NR29 5BP

Although the Pleasure Boat Inn is the preferred launch site for Hickling, it is possible to launch at Catfield Dyke. While not ideal due to its lack of parking and bumpy footpath to the staithe, it is an option. Avoid the private moorings close to the road and launch from the public staithe just beyond. Short or lightweight canoes and kayaks are best suited to this location, longer or heavier boats will be best carried between two people or on a trolley. Once you are waterside, the small vertical drop and presence of a little ladder make launching easy. There is a grassy area here and you are surrounded by trees that make it an idyllic spot for a picnic.

Directions

From Norwich/Wroxham – as you head north out of Hoveton on the A1150 you approach a set of double roundabouts. Take the A1062 (Horning Road) and follow the signs for Horning, Ludham and finally Great Yarmouth until you reach the junction with the A149 to either Stalham or Great Yarmouth. Turn left towards Stalham and after a mile you come to a staggered crossroads with the road to the right signposted for Hickling and Hickling Broad. Turn right here onto Potter Heigham Road and follow this until you come to a road joining from the left, opposite a small red postbox and trackway on your right. Access to the public launch area is beyond the parish staithe, either via the footpath after the yellow thatched cottage down the track by the postbox, or via a small grassy area before the gated access to private parking.

From Great Yarmouth – leave Great Yarmouth on the A149 and follow the signs for Potter Heigham and Cromer. Drive over Potter Heigham Bridge and past the turning left towards Ludham and Horning, and about a mile further on you reach the staggered crossroads as detailed above.

24 Horsey Mill

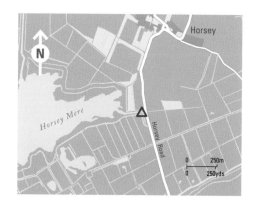

OS Explorer OL40 Grid Ref: TG 456 222
Postcode: NR29 4EF

Horsey Mill is a great starting point if you are looking for either a birdwatching trip on the water or a longer paddle exploring Horsey Mere or Meadow Dyke, the wonderful, narrow, reed-lined channel that winds its way through to Hickling Broad. Parking here is plentiful and the pay and display is excellent value. Parking is of course free for National Trust members. There is a small charge payable for launching, but only if the water bailiff is present. The car park is close to the water and a small vertical drop of only around 50cm makes launching

📷 *Catfield Staithe.*

📷 *Horsey Mill.*

and recovery easy. There is ample space for a picnic with toilets available nearby and the little refreshment hut sells a good selection of food and drinks.

If that is not enough and you have the time, why not have a look round the windmill as well. Paddling on Horsey Mere is not permitted between 1st November and 1st March due to its importance for migratory wildfowl.

Directions

From Wroxham/Hoveton – head north out of Hoveton on the A1150 to a set of double roundabouts. Take the A1062 (Horning Road) and follow the signs for Horning, Ludham and then finally Great Yarmouth until you are on the A149 passing over Potter Heigham Bridge. Once over the bridge drive through the village of Repps with Bastwick, past the right turn for Clippesby and Oby. Shortly after you will come to a crossroads with the left turn signposted towards Martham and Winterton. Turn left here and drive through the village of Martham and continue until you reach the junction with The Lion pub on your right. Turn left here and follow the road through West Somerton. At the next junction go straight on past the village staithe and out into the fields once again. Horsey Mill is around a mile and a half further on.

From Norwich – take the A47 towards Acle. At the Acle roundabout take the second exit onto the A1064 signposted towards Caister-on-Sea and soon you will come to a left turn onto the B1151 signposted for Martham and Winterton. After crossing the A149 you reach Martham, then follow the directions as above.

Great Yarmouth – leave Great Yarmouth on the A149 and follow the signs for Potter Heigham and Cromer. After passing through Ormsby and then Rollesby you will come to a crossroads with the right turn signposted towards Martham and Winterton. Turn right here and follow the directions as above.

25 West Somerton

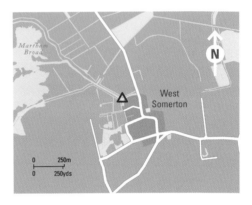

OS Explorer OL40 Grid Ref: TG 467 199
Postcode: NR29 4AB

Although a parish-owned staithe and car park, this is still a viable launching point. The general public are permitted to use the car park, however if you are launching from here please use the Broads Authority 24 hour moorings only a short distance away along the river. From the parish car park walk along the road to the other side of the staithe. Follow the water-side footpath to the Broads Authority moorings.

This is a beautiful stretch of the Thurne to paddle, particularly in the late summer and early autumn. If the light is right, be prepared for some spectacular photo opportunities with the wind pumps along the way.

Directions

From Wroxham/Hoveton – as you head north out of Hoveton on the A1150 you approach a set of double roundabouts. Take the A1062 (Horning Road) and follow the signs for Horning, Ludham and then finally Great Yarmouth until you are on the A149 passing over Potter Heigham Bridge. Once over the bridge drive through the village of Repps with Bastwick, past the right turning for Clippesby and Oby. Shortly after you will come to a crossroads with the left turn signposted towards Martham and Winterton. Turn left here and drive through the village of Martham and continue until you reach the junction with the Lion pub on your right. Turn left here and follow the road into West Somerton and the car park is on the left as you exit the village.

From Norwich – take the A47 towards Acle. As you reach the Acle roundabout take the second exit onto the A1064 signposted towards Caister-on-Sea and soon you will come to a left turn onto the B1151 signposted for Martham and Winterton. After crossing over the A149 you start to drive through Martham, then simply follow the directions as above.

Great Yarmouth – leave Great Yarmouth on the A149 and follow the signs for Potter Heigham and Cromer. After passing through Ormsby and then Rollesby you will come to a crossroads with the right turn signposted towards Martham and Winterton. Turn right here and follow the directions as above.

26 Martham

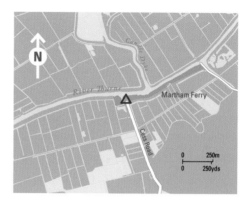

| OS Explorer OL40 Grid Ref: TG 438 191 |
| Postcode: NR29 4RF |

A friendly welcome is assured at Martham Boats. This is the perfect starting point for kayak fishermen wanting to try for one of the famous big Thurne pike or a longer paddle into the large open water of Hickling Broad and Horsey Mere. The boatyard here has recently improved the car parking and has toilets on site as well. The pay and display parking is very reasonably priced with cheap all day rates and a small fee to launch your own canoe or kayak is payable at the reception. Canoe hire can be arranged here as well.

Directions

From Wroxham/Hoveton – as you head north out of Hoveton on the A1150 you approach a set of double roundabouts. Take the A1062 (Horning Road) and follow the signs for Horning, Ludham and then finally Great Yarmouth until you are on the A149 passing over Potter Heigham Bridge. Once over the bridge drive

📷 *Martham Boats' Slip.*

through the village of Repps with Bastwick, past the right turning for Clippesby and Oby. Shortly after you come to a crossroads with the left turn signposted towards Martham and Winterton. Driving up the hill you soon come to a road joining from the left. Turn left here onto Low Road, follow the road round the sharp right-hand bend and turn left at the next junction onto Cess Road. Continue down this road, take the left fork where the road splits, and you will soon reach the boatyard by the river.

From Norwich – take the A47 towards Acle. As you reach the Acle roundabout take the second exit onto the A1064 signposted towards Caister-on-Sea and soon you will come to a left turn onto the B1151 signposted for Martham and Winterton. After crossing over the A149 you start to drive through Martham, then follow the directions as above.

Great Yarmouth – leave Great Yarmouth on the A149 and follow the signs for Potter Heigham and Cromer. After passing through Ormsby and then Rollesby you will come to a cross-roads with the right turn signposted towards

Martham and Winterton. Turn right here and follow the directions as above.

---

27 Potter Heigham Bridge

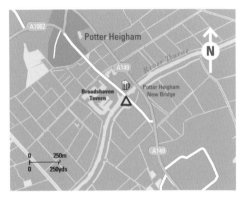

OS Explorer OL40 Grid Ref: TG 420 184
Postcode: NR29 5JQ

Getting onto the water at Potter Heigham is fairly easy as the pay and display car parking at the back of Harry's restaurant is only around 50 metres from the water. At the entry to the car park, look across the road and you will see Phoenix Boat Hire opposite. These chaps are happy for paddlers to launch, and will even help you out onto the water in return for a donation towards keeping their stocks of tea and biscuits going. You have the option of either a vertical drop-in of only around 20cm or alternatively there is a slipway. Launching at Potter Heigham Bridge can be a little tricky, as once you are on the water access under the bridge is narrow, allowing only one boat at a time through, and motor boats can sometimes be travelling pretty fast as they pass

Potter Heigham Bridge.

Potter Heigham parking.

under the bridge. Being an extremely popular location for cruisers and day boats in the summer months, this can lead to something of a bottleneck. Add boats moving to and from the moorings into the mix and it adds up to paddlers needing their wits about them.

Directions

From Wroxham/Hoveton – as you head north out of Hoveton on the A1150 you approach a set of double roundabouts. Take the A1062 (Horning Road) and follow the signs for Horning, Ludham and then finally Great Yarmouth. On entering Potter Heigham follow the sign for The River and Boatyards. This will bring you to the old medieval bridge just past Lathams store. Drive over the bridge and take the first left just past Harry's restaurant into the car park.

From Great Yarmouth – leave Great Yarmouth on the A149 and follow the signs for Potter Heigham and Cromer. After driving through the village of Bastwick you once more enter the 50mph zone and will see a road joining from the left. Turn left here onto the Causeway

and follow the road until you see the traffic lights for the bridge. As you approach the bridge, turn right just before Harry's restaurant into the car park.

---

28 Repps with Bastwick

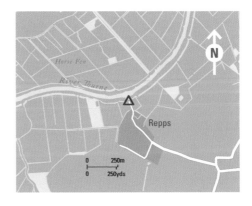

OS Explorer OL40 Grid Ref: TG 413 174
Postcode: NR29 5JU

The staithe at Repps provides an alternative launching point in the Potter Heigham area if others are busy. Car parking is roadside and if you have a low-slung car don't try to go to the very end as the hump-back bridge will catch you out (believe me, I've been a victim). Launching can be either the small vertical drop-in or using the slipway.

Directions

From Wroxham/Hoveton – as you head north out of Hoveton on the A1150 you approach a set of double roundabouts. Take the A1062 (Horning Road) and follow the signs for Horning, Ludham and then finally Great Yarmouth until you are on the A149 passing over Potter Heigham Bridge. Once over the bridge you will enter the village of Repps with Bastwick and come to a crossroads with a signpost for Clippesby, Oby and the B1151 just beyond. Turn right here onto Church Road, and after just under half a mile you come to a sharp right then left bend, and almost immediately a right turn after the farm. Turn right here onto Staithe Road and continue past Willowcroft Campsite to the car parking and staithe a few hundred metres further on.

From Norwich/Great Yarmouth – take the A47 towards Acle. As you reach the Acle roundabout take the exit onto the A1064 signposted towards Caister-on-Sea. Soon you will come to a left turn onto the B1151 for Martham and North Walsham. Turn left here and continue along the road until just past the right turn signposted towards Martham and Winterton. Here you should see a left turn opposite a house with telegraph poles running alongside. Turn left here and follow the road past the church, then turn right at the next junction, and then almost immediately left

onto Staithe Road. The staithe is at the end of the road.

29 Ludham / Womack Staithe

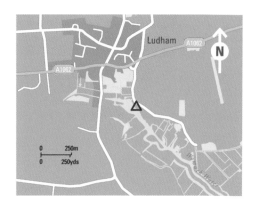

OS Explorer OL40 Grid Ref: TG 391 180

Postcode: NR29 5QG

Ludham Staithe is a very pleasant location, but can be a challenge for the paddler to access. The moorings here are very popular and the cruisers moor together stern-on to the bank. This can make it almost impossible to even see the water let alone get onto it. Paddlers are more likely to be successful using canoes here rather than kayaks, as you can get in and out of them from the ends rather than just having a central cockpit. Using the staithe as a waypoint is a much better idea as it has excellent open and shaded grassy areas for picnics with benches, but you may still find it difficult to land. There is also a small shop at the end of the staithe that sells some refreshments and ice creams.

Directions

From Norwich, Wroxham/Hoveton – as you head north out of Hoveton on the A1150 you approach a set of double roundabouts. Take the A1062 (Horning Road) signposted towards Horning. Continue on this road past the village of Horning and over Ludham Bridge bringing you shortly into the village of Ludham itself. As you drive through the village centre and navigate the sharp left/right by the Kings Arms pub, you soon come to a right turn signposted towards Womack Staithe. Turn right here onto Horsefen Road and the car parking and staithe are only a couple of hundred metres further on.

From Great Yarmouth – leave Great Yarmouth on the A149 and follow the signs for Potter Heigham and Cromer. Shortly after passing over Potter Heigham Bridge, turn left onto the A1062 and follow the signs for Horning and Ludham. Approaching the village, and almost immediately after you pass the 30mph and Ludham signs, take the first left by the one way sign. Turn left at the next junction onto Horsefen Road and car parking and the staithe are only a couple of hundred metres further on.

[📷] *Ludham Staithe.*

30 Thurne Dyke

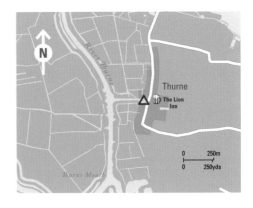

OS Explorer OL40 Grid Ref: TG 403 158

Postcode: NR29 3AP

Launching at Thurne requires that you park in the Lion Inn car park, so please be a patron and try some of their excellent food and drink. Launching here is either by vertical drop-in or there is a parish staithe that paddlers can use for a small donation. You may see the parking area down the access road for the staithe, but this is for parishioners only and expressly for the use of loading and unloading grain (a local by-law that has little bearing now but the sign still stands!).

Directions

From Wroxham/Hoveton – as you head north out of Hoveton on the A1150 you approach a set of double roundabouts. Take the A1062 (Horning Road) and follow the signs for Horning, Ludham and then finally Great Yarmouth until you are on the A149 passing over Potter Heigham Bridge. Once over the bridge you will enter the village of Repps with Bastwick and soon come to a junction with a centre lane for right turns only which is signposted towards Clippesby and Oby. Turn right here onto the B1151 and follow for around a mile and a half where you will come to a crossroads with the right turn signposted for Thurne and Oby. Turn right here and continue all the way into Thurne village. As you enter the village the road bends sharply to the right, shortly after which you will see the dyke on your left. Car parking at the Lion Inn is on your right just after the dyke.

From Norwich/Great Yarmouth – take the A47 towards Acle. As you reach the Acle roundabout take the exit onto the A1064 signposted towards Caister-on-Sea and soon you will come to a left turn onto the B1151 for Martham and North Walsham. Turn left here and after a little over a mile you will come to a crossroads with the left turn signposted for Thurne and Oby. Turn left here and follow the directions as above.

[📷] *Bankside on the River Thurne.*

River Wensum

31 New Mills – Norwich

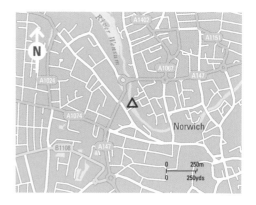

OS Explorer OL40 Grid Ref: TG 226 090
Postcode: NR3 3AH

The start of the Broads area for the city of Norwich, New Mills is best paddled by either getting dropped off close to the launch point or paddling it on a Sunday. The parking restrictions on the roads close to the launch point are not applicable on a Sunday, and with no realistic alternate parking it makes launching here tricky at other times. The launch point is on the northern side of the river and involves carrying your boat down a flight of steps to get to river level. If you can manage this, then the paddle through the city can be superb and a fascinating journey through history.

Alternatively, if you find the steps at this location awkward, a few minutes away there is a slipway at Friar Quay. (OS Explorer OL40 Grid Ref: TG 231 089 / Postcode: NR3 1ES)

Directions

On the Norwich inner ring road, head towards the eastern side of the city for the crossroads with the A1074 Dereham Road. At this point turn into St Benedicts Street which immediately becomes St Swithins Road. After only a couple of hundred metres, turn left and then left again as though you are going back out towards the inner ring road. Just past the St Benedicts car park for Toys R Us and TK Maxx the parking restrictions on the road are not in effect on a Sunday. This is the best time to use this launching point. Simply walk down the New Mills Road which is more like an alley, over the old mill, and the launching steps are on your right.

📷 *The Red Lion at Bishop Bridge.*

32 The Red Lion – Norwich

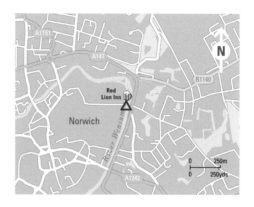

OS Explorer OL40 Grid Ref: TG 239 090

Postcode: NR1 4AA

The Red Lion welcomes paddlers who wish to start their journey from in the city. You can pay a small fee in the pub and park all day, great for those who don't cherish the idea of a lengthy paddle just to tour the short stretch of river through Norwich itself. Be sure you check with the staff in the pub so you get the car parking correct and avoid a penalty fine. A friendly welcome is assured, with the promise of good food and drink once your paddling is over.

Directions

On the Norwich inner ring road, head towards the northern side of the city, over the St Crispins Road flyover and past the Anglia Square Shopping Centre. Take the third exit at the next roundabout onto Whitefriars with the signpost to the Magdalen Street car park. After crossing the river, take the first turning on your left onto St Martin at Palace Plain. Stay on this road following it through a series of bends until you come to the Red Lion at Bishop Bridge.

River Yare

33 Cary's Meadow

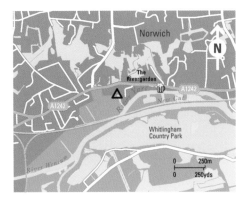

OS Explorer OL40 Grid Ref: TG 252 084

Postcode: NR7 0DU

This is a new launch close to the city that is a great addition for paddlers living in the area. Cary's Meadow car parking area, while small with space for three cars, is directly opposite the Broadland Council Offices, making it very easy to find. Several kissing gates need negotiating, although these do have wooden gates next to them so getting a boat over is not too difficult. A 200m portage to the water follows – watch out for cows and their deposits.

Both the car parking area and launching point are being upgraded with a paddler-specific slipway being installed, so Cary's Meadow will become a great launch point from which to access this stretch of the river. Paddling out from the launch brings you out onto the Yare just inside the Thorpe Loop close to the railway bridge opposite Whitlingham Broad.

Directions

From the A47 – leave the A47 at the Postwick junction and follow the signs for the A1042 and Norwich centre. Continue straight over the next three roundabouts and along Yarmouth Road. At the next set of traffic lights go straight on – the river will be on your left. After several pubs there will be another set of traffic lights and a sign for the ring road opposite the Broadland Council offices. Turn left after this sign into the small car park area.

34 Thorpe St Andrew

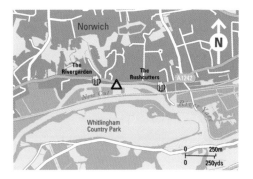

OS Explorer OL40 Grid Ref: TG 260 083

Postcode: NR7 0EW

A great place to start your paddle into Norwich. Launching here is easy with a small vertical drop-in and a slipway that is undergoing renovation by the Broads Authority. This little backwater channel sees few motorised boats so it is ideal for beginners. Parking is roadside and can be busy, but the portage to the water is only 50 metres. Be careful if you park here as this is one of the main roads into Norwich.

Directions

From Norwich city centre take the A1242 Yarmouth Road out towards the A47. You will pass several pubs on your right, including The Rivergarden. Just beyond these is the launching point and slipway. Park along the road or by the slipway, simply cross the road to the river. From the A47 – leave the A47 via the Postwick junction and follow the signs for the A1242 towards Norwich city centre. Pass the Rushcutters pub on your left – the launch spot is easy to see through the trees on your left just after.

---

35 Whitlingham Broad

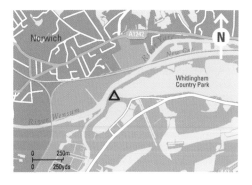

OS Explorer OL40 Grid Ref: TG 250 078
Postcode: NR14 8TR

Whitlingham Broad access for paddlers is a great example of the type of facilities that should be in place for those wanting to get onto the Broads in canoes and kayaks. An excellent floating pontoon awaits paddlers who make the long trek from the car park past the outdoor education centre. The ramp for the pontoon is a few metres past the entrance

Whitlingham Broad pontoon.

to the centre. The paddle from here into and through Norwich is well worth the walk. Alternatively if you drive about 150m further on you will come across the Visitor Centre – you can park here and launch onto the broad. You must first obtain permission to go onto the Broad from the Whitlingham Adventure centre.

Directions

Finding Whitlingham is very easy. Follow the Norwich inner ring road to the Norfolk County Council building roundabout and follow the signpost for Trowse. You will also see the brown signs for the country park and ski slope. After the railway bridge you soon come to a left turn onto Whitlingham Lane, still following the brown signs for the country park. Continue along this road until some speed bumps appear in the road. Shortly after the first bumps the car park is well signposted on your left.

From the A47 – leave the A47 at the Trowse junction with the A146 and head towards Norwich. Keep in the right-hand lane of the dual carriageway as you pass through the traffic lights and approach the roundabout. Take the third exit, noting the brown signs for the country park, and follow the directions as above.

---

36 Whitlingham Woods Car Park

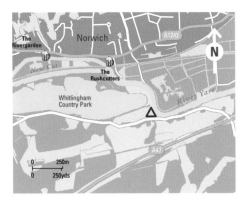

OS Explorer OL40 Grid Ref: TG 269 078
Postcode: NR14 8TS

Another newly-improved launch point on the Yare close to the city. Here there is ample pay and display car parking close to the water, with the added bonus of picnic facilities and a small play area for the kids. Don't be tempted to park on the road as you will get a fairly expensive ticket. It is a bankside vertical drop-in that is ideal for those wanting to paddle up into the city from a little further afield.

Directions
From the A47 – leave the A47 at the Trowse junction and head down the dual carriageway towards the city and ring road. Try to be in the right-hand lane before you get to the traffic lights, or move into it as soon as possible after you have turned right and passed the petrol station on your right. At the roundabout take the third exit signposted for Trowse. Head over the bridge and take the second left onto Whitlingham Lane. This is signposted as a dead-end and also the home of the ski slope; yes we have a ski slope in Norfolk! Drive down Whitlingham Lane watching out for the speed bumps, and after passing the broad on your left you will soon come to the car park for Whitlingham Woods on your right.

From Norwich City ring road – drive around the inner ring road and head towards Trowse and the Norwich County Hall. At the roundabout take the turning towards Trowse and follow the directions as above.

---

37 Bramerton Common

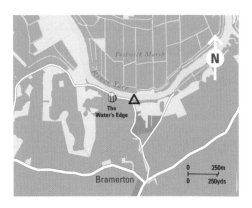

OS Explorer OL40 Grid Ref: TG 294 060
Postcode: NR14 7ED

Bramerton Common is a pleasant launching point from which to explore this section of river. Launching is straightforward with a small ladder present a short distance from the car parking area, should you need it. Otherwise the one metre vertical drop-in is comfortable for those in open canoes and sit-on-tops, but slightly trickier for kayaks. The river here is fairly wide and is very pleasant in the summer months.

Directions

From Wroxham/Norwich – take the A47 to the Trowse junction and head towards Beccles. Almost immediately, at the next set of traffic lights, take the filter lane off to the left onto Kirby Road signposted towards Bramerton and Rockland St Mary. Follow the road for around three miles and you come to a junction signposted for Surlingham as the road bends round to the right with white fences opposite. Turn left here onto Surlingham Road and take the second left turn onto Mill Hill signposted for Woods End. Around half a mile from here you will come to the River Yare and Bramerton Common car park on your right, with the Woods End pub a short distance further on.

From Beccles – take the A146 towards Norwich where shortly after passing a van and car dealership on your left, you come to a staggered crossroads and central lane for turning, with the road to the right signposted for Slade Road. Turn right here and follow this road going straight across the next crossroads, and then turn right at the following junction with barns opposite and a signpost for Bramerton. Turn left at the next junction, signposted for Surlingham as the road bends

round to the right with white fences opposite, and follow the directions as above.

38 Postwick Wharf

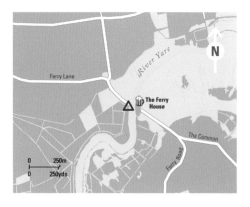

OS Explorer OL40 Grid Ref: TG 307 075
Postcode: NR13 5DU

Opposite the Ferry Inn pub, this is a great launching point for exploring this section of the Yare. The majority of launching points along the Yare are only accessible from the southern side of the river, so Postwick Wharf is ideal for those who live, or are staying, north of the River Yare and are looking for a launching point close by. The access to the river is a track that is not in the best of condition, so this launching point is not for those with a low vehicle. A vertical drop-in of around one metre makes launching canoes easy, while a small beach and inlet just to the right is perfect for kayaks. This inlet is quite overgrown and a little investment would encourage paddlers to launch from here. Car parking is limited with enough space for around ten cars.

Directions

From Wroxham/Norwich – take the A47 to the Brundall roundabout. Take the third exit onto Cucumber Lane signposted for Brundall. Follow this road until you come to a sharp left-hand bend with Postwick Lane joining from the right. Turn onto Postwick Lane and follow this road out through the houses and into fields until you pass a crossroads sign and then some very large farm buildings of breezeblocks and slatted wood on your right. Just beyond these is the crossroads. Take the left turn onto the road passing a 'Weak Bridge 240 yards ahead' sign. This is Church Road and you soon come to a sharp right-hand bend with a wooden gate adjoining. Almost immediately after this bend the track turning is on your left. Although this is only a track, it is fairly well maintained and at the end of it you will find the wharf.

From Great Yarmouth – take the A47 towards Acle and then Norwich. At the Brundall

[📷] *Pit stop on the River Yare. Photo | Mark Rainsley.*

roundabout take the second exit onto Cucumber Lane and follow the directions as above.

---

39 Rockland Broad

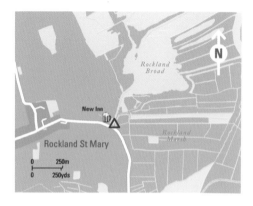

OS Explorer OL40 Grid Ref: TG 327 046
Postcode: NR14 7HP

Rockland Broad is a great place to paddle, especially if you are just starting out and want easy access and calm, quiet waters. Parking here is free and very close to the water, with both a vertical drop-in and a slipway. Donations are requested for use of the slip.

A short paddle out gets you onto the wide, open water of the broad with its many areas to explore. There is also access from here out onto the Yare if you feel like exploring further afield. This area is great for wildlife and having an adventure. There is also The New Inn right by the launching point should you need refreshing after your paddle.

Directions

From Wroxham/Norwich – take the A47 to the

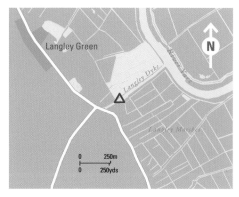

Rockland Broad slipway.

Trowse junction and head towards Beccles. Almost immediately, at the next set of traffic lights, take the filter lane off to the left onto Kirby Road signposted towards Bramerton and Rockland St Mary. Follow the road through the village of Bramerton and into Rockland St Mary. As you drive through the village you pass a left turn signposted towards Surlingham and pass the few remaining houses before finding yourself back on a tree-lined stretch of the road. The entry to the car park in only a few hundred metres further on your left. If you reach The New Inn pub, you've missed it.

From Beccles – take the A146 towards Norwich and as you enter the section passing the village of Thurton you come to a couple of right turns. The first is signposted towards Low Common and the second to Ashby St Mary. Turn right here onto Ashby Road and continue until you come to a junction. Turn left and then almost immediately right onto Church Lane. Stay on this narrow road as you pass St Andrews thatched church on your right and navigate the tight bends before reaching the next junction. Turn left here signposted to-wards Rockland and Norwich and after half a mile you will pass The New Inn on your left and the staithe on your right, and then see the right turning into the Broads Authority car park.

40 Langley Staithe

OS Explorer OL40 Grid Ref: TG 365 027
Postcode: NR14 6AD

Hidden away down a gated track, Langley Staithe is a real find. Langley Dyke was originally cut in medieval times, to allow boats bringing stone access to the building site of a Benedictine priory. The remains are still visible among the nearby farm buildings. Its well-maintained Broads Authority 24-hour mooring allows the easiest of launches onto some beautiful, scenic water. Dragonflies and damselflies are in abundance and those who would like to experience this stretch of the Yare, but are not too sure of launching directly onto it, will enjoy the gentle, tree-lined dyke that stretches for about half a kilometre before opening onto the Yare.

Directions

From Norwich – there are two routes to Langley, one via the A146 to Loddon and back on yourself up to Langley, and one a more scenic route via the Kirby Road through the local villages. As the scenery is part of the enjoyment, this is the route I will describe. Leaving Norwich, take the A146 towards Loddon and Beccles at the A47 Trowse junction. At the second set of traffic lights, turn left signposted for Claxton, Surlingham and several other villages onto Kirby Road. Follow this road through Bramerton, Rockland St Mary, and Claxton, passing the Beauchamp Arms pub signs and finally entering Langley Green. As you approach a small monument where the road bends to the right, take the left (or seemingly straight on) turn onto Langley Street and then the first left. This is a gravelled track with wooden gate that leads to the staithe parking area. The drop-in is only a short walk further on.

From Beccles – take the A146 towards Norwich and the first right turn for Loddon, shortly after the BP petrol station. Continue through Loddon until the road bends left, with a road joining on the right and a wooden bus shelter marking the spot. Take the right turn onto Langley Road and continue until you come to the monument. Turn right here and take the first left onto the gravel road to the staithe.

---

41 Cantley Staithe

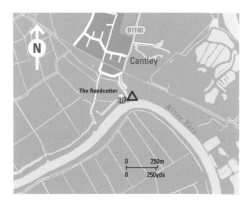

OS Explorer OL40 Grid Ref: TG 382 034

Postcode: NR13 3SH

Cantley Staithe has recently been renovated and is now a great place to launch and explore this area of the Yare. Standing next to the sugar factory, the staithe features a

Langley Dyke.

Cantley Staithe.

superb combination of slipway and small vertical drop-in along the moorings and floating pontoons. Whatever form of canoe, kayak, sit-on-top or inflatable you have, you will find launching here very easy. Parking is opposite the access road for the slipway and is well-signposted before the pub car park. Be aware that waterskiing is permitted on the stretch of river upstream towards Brundall at certain times. In the summer this is from 16.00 until sunset, while in the winter it is 09.00 until sunset on every day except Sunday when it is permitted between 13.00 and sunset.

Directions

From Norwich – take the A47 towards Acle until you have just passed through the single carriageway section past Brundall. As the road once again becomes dual carriageway you pass a series of signs on your left, firstly for Reedham and The Broads, then a left turn towards Wroxham and North Walsham. Just as you come out of the 50mph speed restriction, a right turn only lane appears signposted towards Cantley and Beighton. Turn right here onto the B1140 Acle Road and take the first left onto Cox Hill Road signposted for Cantley. This road will take you through the village of Beighton, past the Cock Tavern and around a series of sharp left then right bends where you then enter Cantley itself. Once over the level crossing, take the right fork and then immediately left following the sign for the staithe.

From Great Yarmouth – take the A47 towards Acle, and then towards Norwich once you

have reached the Acle roundabout. After just under two miles you enter a 50mph zone and soon see a road to your left signposted towards Cantley and Beighton on the B1140. Turn right here and follow the directions as above.

---

42 Reedham

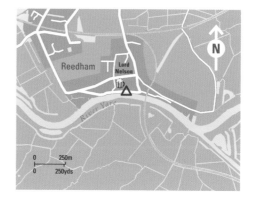

OS Explorer OL40 Grid Ref: TG 419 016
Postcode: NR13 3TE

Very few paddlers visit this area as the river here can be subject to some fairly strong tidal forces. If you are looking to paddle this part of the Yare you need to be very aware of the

Reedham.

local tide times and river levels. The stretch of the Yare between here and Cadge's Drainage Mill close to Breydon Water is also a water-skiing area (see Cantley Staithe for details) so be aware. Launching at Reedham is fairly easy. The vertical drop-in from the moorings can fluctuate with the river levels but around 50cm is fairly common. Parking is free and there are plenty of spaces along the water front. The Nelson Inn provides a great place for post-paddle refreshment.

Directions

From Norwich – take the A47 towards Acle and take the first exit for the village before you get to the roundabout. If you reach the roundabout, don't panic, just take the first exit and go through the village. You'll come to the roundabout for Reedham that way. As you come up the slip road off the A47 you come to a roundabout. Take the second exit following the signs for Pettitts Animal Adventure Park and Reedham. At the next roundabout, turn right onto Reedham Road and follow this through the countryside until you pass over the railway bridge and see a road on your left signposted towards Reedham. Turn right here until just after the next sharp left-hand bend where you see the road almost forks, with a memorial in between. Take the road on the right onto Riverside and park along the river.

From Great Yarmouth – take the A47 towards Acle until you pass the Stracey Arms windmill on your right. Take the next left onto Branch Road and drive into and through Halvergate.

At the junction with Lower Green Road turn right towards Reedham. Head over the railway bridge and follow the directions as above.

If you are travelling from the Beccles direction, there is a ferry at Reedham which runs from 7.30 a.m. to 10.00 p.m. Monday to Fridays and 8.00 a.m. to 10.00 p.m. Saturdays and Sundays, summer and winter alike. It is the only river crossing between Norwich and Great Yarmouth and can save a significant amount of travel time if you are staying locally.

River Chet

43 Loddon Staithe

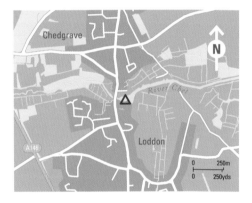

Overflow stream from Hardley Flood.

The Chet is a very pleasant paddle with a great deal of wildlife living on, in and around it. To explore the full length of this part of the Chet you can launch at Loddon Staithe. Here you will find a small pay and display car park directly next to the river with the first two hours parking free. Launching is via a small vertical drop of around 50cm next to the footbridge, but be aware of the remains of old wooden pilings just beneath the water surface close to the footbridge. Public toilets are also available at the car park. Starting here and paddling its full length brings you onto the River Yare with The Ferry Inn at Reedham Ferry only 500m downstream, presenting an ideal opportunity for a day trip with a pleasant pub lunch before the return paddle.

Directions

From Norwich/A47 – from the A47 at Trowse take the exit signposted for Lowestoft and Norwich. Follow the A146 signs for Lowest-

📷 *River Chet.*

oft towards Beccles. Continue straight on through the first set of traffic lights and along the Loddon Road through Thurton. Shortly after Thurton you will see a sign on your left towards Loddon and Chedgrave. Take this left turn and follow the road into Loddon. The speed limit changes from 30 to 20 as you enter the village, and you soon see the impressive white, wooden building on the right which was the old mill. After this you will see the car park sign on the left for the launching point.

From Beccles – continue along the A146 from Beccles and take the first right turn signposted for Loddon and Chedgrave. Continue into and through Loddon passing the church and village centre. Shortly after you will see the car park sign for the launching point on your right.

44 Pyes Mill

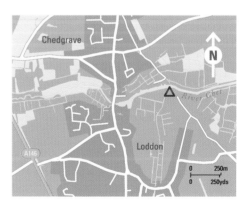

This is an alternative launching point for Loddon which is especially useful if the small car park in the village is full. By launching from here you are only missing out on around a quarter of a mile of water between here and the village, easily added if you've got time at the end of your paddle. Be aware that the car park has a 6'6" height restriction.

Don't try to launch where the boats moor-up as the drop can be too great. Instead the river can be accessed via a small channel – go through the picnic tables near the car park entrance and down the bank to the small channel that links to the river.

Directions

From Norwich/A47 – from the A47 at Trowse take the exit signposted for Lowestoft and Norwich. Follow the A146 signs for Lowestoft towards Beccles. Continue straight on through the first set of traffic lights and along the Loddon Road through Thurton. Continue around the Loddon bypass until you see a sign for the Loddon Industrial Estate heading left. Take this left turn and follow the road until you come to a sharp left-hand bend with a road joining from the right with a small triangle of grassy island. This is Norton Road, a short distance down here you take a left into Mill Road. At the end of Mill Road, turn left and continue to the car park at the end. However, be aware of the height restriction if you have boats on the roof.

From Beccles – continue along the A146 from Beccles and take the first right turn signposted for the Loddon Industrial Estate. Follow the directions as above.

River Waveney

45 Shotford Bridge (Harleston)

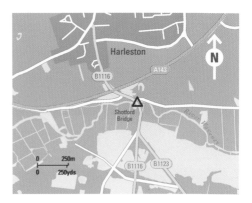

OS Explorer 230 Grid Ref: TM 246 822
Postcode: IP20 9QT

This is the start for a real canoeing adventure. The Waveney here is shallow, narrow and winding but well worth exploring. Launching at Shotford Bridge can be tricky due to the launch point needing some repair. Launch from either bank using the wooden platforms available. If you are launching from the southern bank, be careful using the stile and beware of the foundations of the old bridge in the river bed as you paddle off.

Directions

From Norwich – leave Norwich and the A47 by the Trowse junction and then turn right at the traffic lights onto the B1332 towards Bungay and Poringland. Follow this road all the way past Ditchingham until you reach the roundabout with the A143. Take the third exit onto the A143 and follow this road towards Harleston. At the first roundabout go straight over following the sign for Harleston Industrial Estate. Stay on the A143 past the turning for the industrial estate and make note shortly after of the road on your left (with the no left turn sign); this is the road you need. Continue to the roundabout and go all the way around so you are travelling back the way you have just come. Take the first turning on your right signposted to Fressingfield. Drive down this road and turn right at the junction and then almost immediately left. Park on the right-hand side of the road under the trees.

From Thetford – take the A1066 and then the A143 past Diss towards Harleston. At the first roundabout for Harleston, continue straight over and take the first turning on the right signposted towards Fressingfield and follow the directions as above.

[📷] *Shotford Bridge launching point.*

46 Homersfield Bridge

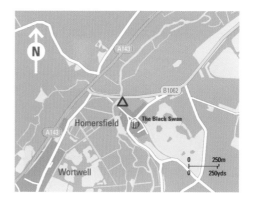

OS Explorer 231 Grid Ref: TM 283 857
Postcode: IP20 0ET

A great place to start paddling from with plenty of free parking on either side of the bridge. Wooden platforms make getting in and out of the river easy and with the Black Swan pub a few metres away, it also makes this an ideal place for a break and refreshment. If parking on the north side of the bridge (Wortwell) beware of the height restriction on entering the car park.

Directions

From Norwich – leave Norwich and the A47 by the Trowse junction and then turn right at the traffic lights onto the B1332 towards Bungay and Poringland. Follow this road all the way past Ditchingham until you reach the roundabout with the A143. Take the third exit onto the A143 and follow this road towards Harleston. Turn left following the signposts for Homersfield, Flixton and the Aviation Museum. The height-restricted car park can be

📷 *Homersfield Bridge.*

47 Bungay Castle

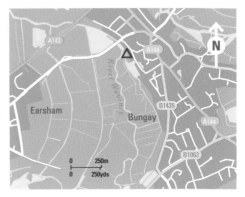

OS Explorer 231 Grid Ref: TM 334 897

Postcode: NR35 1DE

seen on your right. To park on the southern bank with no height restriction, continue past this first car park and take the next right turn signposted Homersfield Village Only and take the first right just after the thatched pink cottages. Parking is next to the Black Swan pub. From Thetford – take the A1066 and then the A143 past Diss towards Harleston. Continue on the A143 passing Harleston and turn right following the signpost for the Aviation Museum and follow the directions as above.

A very small access point onto the Waveney, this location offers the option to paddle the Bungay 'Loop', ideal for those looking for a shorter paddle one way without the start and finish points being far apart. Car parking is very limited on the roadside and the access track running alongside some of the old castle walls is narrow. Bungay Sluice is not far away on the other side of the town and makes a great finishing point.

Directions

From Norwich – leave Norwich and the A47 by the Trowse junction and then turn right at the traffic lights onto the B1332 towards Bungay and Poringland. Follow this road all the way past Ditchingham until you reach the roundabout with the A143. Take the third exit onto the A143 and continue to the next roundabout. Take the first exit onto Broad Street until you come to a town centre roundabout. Here, take

📷 *Black Swan, Homersfield.*

the third exit onto Earsham Road that is also signposted for Norwich and Earsham. Soon this road bends sharply around to the right with a junction straight ahead. Turn off left here avoiding the right-hand bend, and at the end of the multi-coloured houses on your left, turn into the very narrow road of Castle Lane. Park along the right-hand side of the road by the wall and the track can be seen leading to the river. Alternatively, opposite the entrance to Castle Lane is Outney Road. There is limited parking available down here.

From Thetford – take the A1066 and then follow the A143 past Diss and Harleston. Continue on the A143 to Bungay. At the first roundabout take the exit for Bungay, Halesworth and the A144 onto Broad Street and follow the directions as above.

[◎] *Bungay Castle track.*

48 Outney Meadow

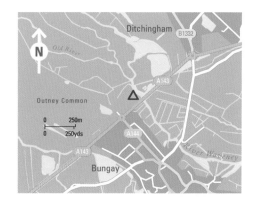

OS Explorer OL40 Grid Ref: TM 333 904
Postcode: NR35 1HG

Outney Meadow is a great place to either camp or simply launch and explore the Bungay area of the Waveney. Outney Meadow is the furthermost upstream launching point on the Waveney within the Broads area. It boasts a wonderful, friendly atmosphere and some idyllic scenery as you either paddle upstream and around the Bungay Loop, or head downstream towards Beccles past Wainford, Ellingham and Geldeston. The launching point is extremely well maintained with a small vertical drop-in from the re-inforced bank.

There is a small fee for launching your own canoes or kayaks, but this does include car parking.

Outney Meadow also has its' own canoes that you can hire on a half or full day basis.

Directions

From Norwich – leave Norwich and the A47 by the Trowse junction and then turn right at the traffic lights onto the B1332 towards Bungay and Poringland. Follow this road past Ditchingham until you reach the roundabout with the A143. Take the third exit onto the A143. After you cross over the river you come to a second roundabout with signs for the A144 to Bungay and Halesworth, and a brown sign for Outney Meadow. Turn right (third exit) at this roundabout and follow the road around to the right where you will find the car park and office for Outney Meadow Caravan Park.

From Thetford – take the A1066 and then the A143 past Diss and Harleston, and at the first Bungay roundabout take the first exit and follow the road around to the right.

📷 *Outney Meadow.*

49 Bungay Sluice

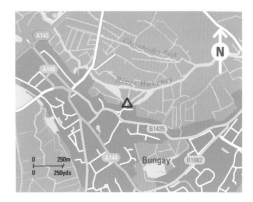

OS Explorer OL40 Grid Ref: TM 340 897

Postcode: NR35 1BF

A perfect location from which to explore this beautiful stretch of the River Waveney; can be a little tricky to find first time out.. Car parking is free but only open between 0700 and 2200. Launching is a breeze with purpose-built portage points on both sides of the sluice. An extremely small vertical drop-in makes launching both canoes and kayaks extremely easy.

Directions

From Norwich – leave Norwich and the A47 by the Trowse junction and then turn right at the traffic lights onto the B1332 towards Bungay and Poringland. Follow this road all the way past Ditchingham until you reach the roundabout with the A143. Go straight across (second exit) into Bungay passing over the river, and at the junction turn sharply left onto Trinity Street. Follow the road as it bends sharply left passing Staithe Close and Trinity Gardens on your left. Take the next left onto Staithe Road

📷 Bungay River Centre.

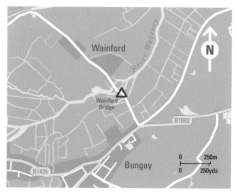

OS Explorer OL40 Grid Ref: TM 350 901

Postcode: NR35 1TA

as you approach a little green with a tree in the centre, and follow the road around as it bends left and passes a large, white wooden building that used to be a mill. Drive over the speed bumps and the car park lies around a hundred metres beyond.

From Lowestoft – take the A143 through Beccles and towards Bungay and follow the instructions as above.

From Thetford – take the A1066 and then the A143, heading past Diss and Harleston. At the first Bungay roundabout take the third exit heading into Bungay. At the junction turn left into Trinity Street and follow the instructions as above.

Wainford Bridge is one of several launching points along this stretch of the Waveney with excellent portage facilities making launching canoes and kayaks easy. Parking is a little limited with space for a few cars along the road. The river here winds its way through some wonderful scenery with open vistas across the river valley and many overhanging trees providing shady relief from the summer sun. A well-marked floating boom protects paddlers and indicates the presence of the sluice.

📷 Bungay Sluice launch and portage east.

📷 Wainford Bridge west portage.

LAUNCHING POINT DESCRIPTIONS BY RIVER

Portage

Paddlers must carry their boats around Wainford Sluice, but the portage points are well marked, built and maintained. The portage distance is approximately 50 metres over grass.

Directions

From Norwich – leave Norwich and the A47 by the Trowse junction and then turn right at the traffic lights onto the B1332 towards Bungay and Poringland. Follow this road all the way past Ditchingham until you reach the roundabout with the A143. Go straight across onto Ditchingham Dam and immediately left onto Pirnhow Street. Follow the road as it bends round to the right and after around a kilometre you come to Wainford Sluice. Parking can be found here along the roadside.

From Lowestoft – follow the A146 towards Beccles and then the A143 to Bungay. At the first roundabout for Bungay, signposted Ditchingham, take the first exit signposted for Wainford Maltings, on to Ditchingham Dam and follow the directions as above.

51 Ellingham Sluice

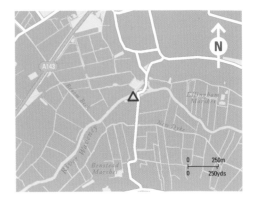

OS Explorer OL40 Grid Ref: TM 364 916
Postcode: NR35 2EX

Access at Ellingham Sluice shows a real contrast on either side. On the upstream side there is another well-signposted and maintained vertical drop-in and portage point. However, downstream across the road the access is hardly maintained and is a very steep 1.5 metre drop to muddy and then shallow water. From this point through to Geldeston Lock the local Bungay Cherry Tree Angling Club have fishing rights, so be aware and courteous to

Wainford Bridge east portage.

Ellingham Bridge portage east.

other river users as you paddle by. Parking is available along the road, but only for a maximum of around three or four cars. A stile can be found along the road around 10 metres to the south of the gated access to the sluice portage points, which makes accessing the river upstream much easier.

Directions

From Norwich – leave Norwich and the A47 by the Trowse junction and then turn right at the traffic lights onto the B1332 towards Bungay and Poringland. Follow this road all the way past Ditchingham until you reach the roundabout with the A143. Go straight across onto Ditchingham Dam and immediately left onto Pirnhow Street. Follow the road as it bends round to the right and after around a kilometre you come to Wainford Sluice. Just before the next junction take the smaller road on the left just after the 'Give Way' sign onto Low Road. After around a kilometre and a half, turn left by the signpost for Ellingham onto the road with the 'Weak Bridge ¾ mile ahead' sign. Ellingham Mill is only a short distance beyond. From Lowestoft – follow the A146 towards Beccles and then the A143 to Bungay. As you drive along the A143, pass the first turning for Ellingham (East) and take the next left by the shooting, riding and fishing shop onto Church Road that is signposted for Ellingham Mill. Continue down Church Road and over the brick bridge, where just on the other side turn right towards the church. Ellingham Mill lies just around the next couple of bends.

52 Geldeston (The Locks Inn)

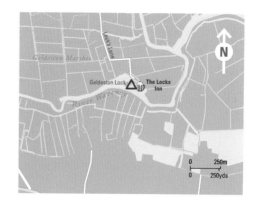

OS Explorer OL40 Grid Ref: TM 389 908
Postcode: NR34 0HS

Surely one of the hidden gems of the Broads, The Locks Inn has the warmest of welcomes combined with great choice of food and drink in a location most pubs can only dream of. The approach to the inn is down a fairly long, and very bumpy, track. Just before you get to the inn itself you come to an open car parking area. This is where the owners would like paddlers to park if they wish to launch. Don't worry as the walk is only around 100 metres to

Mooring at The Locks Inn.

the water. Launching is via a vertical drop-in of a little over one metre but there is a ladder built into the bank which makes it easier for kayaks. While there is no charge for launching at The Locks Inn, as a courtesy please be a patron while you are there – you'll find it difficult to resist and you won't regret it.

Directions

From Norwich – take the A146 towards Beccles, passing Loddon and Hales until you come to the roundabout with the A143 signposted towards Bungay. Turn right here onto the A143 and almost immediately take the first left onto Stockton Road. At the junction turn right and then immediately left onto Geldeston Hill. Follow the road for around 600m and as the road takes a right-hand bend, you will see the sign and turning on your left marked for The Locks Inn.

From Lowestoft/Beccles – take the A146 past Beccles until you come to a left turn just before the roundabout with the A143 signposted towards Gillingham. Follow this road round the left-hand bend and then take the right turn onto The Street, then the first left onto King's Dam. Stay on this road through the village until you enter Dunburgh. Just after The Wherry Inn on your right you come to a junction. Turn left here and the turning for The Locks Inn is around 350m further along on your left.

53 Geldeston (Rowan Craft)

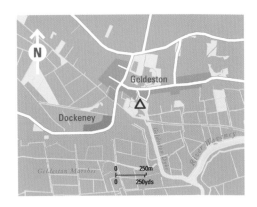

OS Explorer OL40 Grid Ref: TM 389 917

Postcode: NR34 0LY

A warm and friendly welcome awaits paddlers at Rowan Craft and whether you have your own boat to launch or want to hire a canoe for the day, you can be assured of some great advice and service here. A small fee of £6 for launching and £1 for parking is payable. Launching is from Rowan Craft's own slipway and you can park your car close by, so no long walk.

For caravan owners, there are also pitches available here if you want to stay a while.

Opening hours 8.30am to 1pm and 2pm to 5pm.

Directions

From Norwich – leave Norwich and the A47 by the Trowse junction and head past Loddon towards Beccles on the A146. When you reach the roundabout signposted with Diss and Bungay to the right, take this road (the A143), and then take the first left onto Stockton Road. At the next junction, turn right and then immediately left into Geldeston Hill and then left again into The Street. Here you will see The Wherry Inn and turn right into Big Row where you will find Rowan Craft.

From Lowestoft/Beccles – from Beccles, follow the signs for Norwich and the A146. From the A146/Beccles roundabout, continue for just under a mile until you see a left turn just after a couple of signposts indicating 'Weak Bridge' and then 'Services ahead'. Turn left here onto Loddon Road and continue as the road bends sharply to the left. After a couple of hundred metres, turn right into The Street and follow it as it winds its way into the village of Geldeston. Opposite The Wherry Inn, turn left into Big Row and you will find Rowan Craft a short way down here on your right.

From Diss/Bungay – follow the A143 past Bungay and when you reach a sign for Ellingham Mill, Grain Store and Public Weighbridge, turn right onto Church Road. Follow Church Road until just after it enters the village of Geldeston where at a crossroads with roads joining from the left and right, turn right onto The Street and then right again into Big Row opposite The Wherry Inn.

📷 Rowan Craft.

54 Beccles Quay

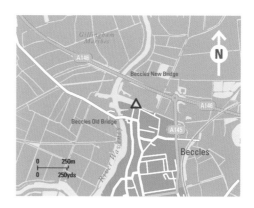

OS Explorer OL40 Grid Ref: TM 423 911
Postcode: NR34 9BH

A good launching point onto the Waveney that gives paddlers a great view of the town. Parking is free for the first 2 hours and then a small fee by the hour or for all day if staying longer. If you are visiting in the busy summer months it pays to get here early. Launching is via a large concrete slipway into a small quay that leads out onto the river itself. Portage to the slipway from the car park is along a well-maintained path of around 150 metres. You then need to cross over the bridge.

📷 Beccles quay slipway.

Alternatively, drop the boat off at the slipway and then park the car. This will save time and effort and negotiating the footbridge.

Directions

From Norwich – at the A47 Trowse junction, take the A146 and follow the signs for Beccles. As you approach Beccles you cross over the river and come to a roundabout. Turn right here onto George Westwood Way, continue past the entrance for Morrisons on your left and take the next right onto Common Lane North where you will see signs for car parking. Take the first right onto Pound Road, follow the left-hand bend onto Fen Lane and take the first right into the car parking for the quay.

From Lowestoft – take the A146 to Beccles. Take the first exit at the roundabout to Beccles. Pass the entrance to Morrisons on the left and then follow the directions as above.

Through Beccles – as you head out of the town towards the roundabout with the A146 and Morrisons, you pass the pedestrian crossing and turn left onto Common Lane North. Then follow the directions above.

55 Waveney River Centre

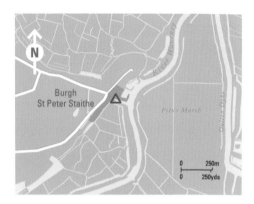

OS Explorer OL40 Grid Ref: TM 492 934
Postcode: NR34 0BT

The Waveney River Centre boasts all the facilities you would expect from a modern, multi award-winning holiday park with the feel of a campsite. Whether you are staying in one of their lodges or caravans, camping in your own tent, or simply visiting for the day to launch onto the Waveney, this is a great starting point from which to explore the Broads. Launching is via either vertical drop-in or slip way and the small launching fee also includes your car parking. Reception is housed within the shop

[📷] *River Waveney from Beccles.*

[📷] *Waveney River Centre.*

and the launching point is only a short walk from the large car park. The river here is wide and Oulton Broad is easily within reach. Also a member of the Broads Hire Association, the centre has a fleet of canoes for hire.

Directions

From Norwich – take the A146 towards Beccles until you reach the roundabout with the A143. Take the first exit towards Great Yarmouth and Haddiscoe and follow the road for just over a mile until you reach a turn off to your right signposted towards Aldeby. Turn right here, follow the road through Aldeby and continue until you pass through Burgh St Peter and reach the Waveney River Centre.

From Lowestoft – take the A146 until you pass Beccles and reach the roundabout with the A143 signposted towards Great Yarmouth. Turn right here onto the A143 and follow the directions to Aldeby as described above.

From Beccles – take the A145 through Beccles, turning left at the roundabout onto the A146. Continue to the roundabout with the A143 and then the directions for Aldeby as above.

56 Oulton Broad

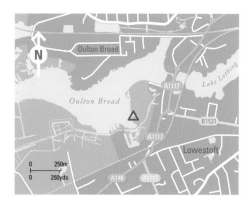

OS Explorer OL40 Grid Ref: TM 518 924
Postcode: NR33 9JR

Oulton Broad is a great place to paddle. It is an interesting, wide expanse of water with plenty of areas to explore. For the novice paddler it is ideal, with a 100m path from the car park to the free slipway. Car parking is plentiful, but is pay and display. Charges are low with good all day rates. These charges change depending on whether it is high or low season, so please check the signs at the pay and display machines. For those wanting a longer paddle there is access onto the Waveney via Oulton

[📷] *Dunburgh, River Waveney.*

[📷] *Oulton Broad.*

Dyke with the Waveney River Centre around 3km away.

Directions

From Norwich – leave Norwich and the A47 at the Trowse junction and take the A146 past Loddon and Beccles following the signposts for Lowestoft. As you approach Lowestoft itself, Oulton Broad and the car park are signposted with large brown signs. After the roundabout by the broad, turn left onto Bridge Road and follow it as it bends round to the left. Drive past The Boulevard with its car park on your right and just beyond the first few shops you will see the entrance into the Nicholas Everett car park with the large blue entrance signs. Continue through the car park until you see the masts of small boats and this is where the slipway is, so park anywhere you can close to this point.

57 Somerleyton Staithe

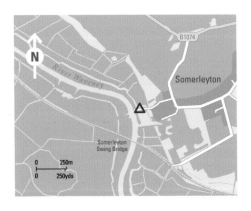

OS Explorer OL40 Grid Ref: TM 475 970

Postcode: NR32 5QR

Not the easiest launching point to find, but still a valuable one to know as a waypoint, Somerleyton is a vertical drop-in of around one metre, however there are several ladders along the staithe that will aid launching and landing. The trickiest part of getting to the waterside by car is as you approach the river-bank. The track is narrow and suddenly rises to a serious hump on which most normal cars will probably bottom out. Only a 4x4 or car with good ground clearance will make it. Parking a car before this hump is tricky as there is little room roadside; after the hump there is space for around four cars.

Directions

From Norwich – leave Norwich and the A47 at the Trowse junction and take the A146 to Loddon. As you pass Loddon you come to the village of Hales where, just after the petrol station, you turn onto the B1136 signposted towards Great Yarmouth and Haddiscoe. Follow this road to the junction with the A143 and turn left towards Great Yarmouth. After a short distance you will cross the river bridge at St Olaves. Just after the bridge, turn left onto the B1074 towards Somerleyton and continue for just over 1.5 miles where you will see a sign for The Duke's Head pub. Turn right here onto Slugs Lane. Just after The Duke's Head turn right down a track and fork right to the river.

From Beccles – leave Beccles on the A146 and at the first roundabout turn onto the A143 towards Great Yarmouth. Continue to St

Olaves and once over the bridge follow the directions as above.

58 St Olaves (The Bell Inn)

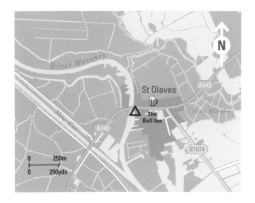

OS Explorer OL40 Grid Ref: TM 458 994
Postcode: NR31 9HE

A great place to launch from and explore this stretch of the Waveney, The Bell Inn openly welcomes paddlers. However, please be sure to park your car away from the pub entrance and take advantage of the friendly welcome and great food and drink on offer inside. Launching is straightforward at the staithe with a small vertical drop-in that is easy for both canoes and kayaks.

Directions

From Norwich – leave Norwich and the A47 at the Trowse junction and take the A146 to Loddon. As you pass Loddon you come to the village of Hales where, just after the petrol station, you turn onto the B1136 signposted towards Great Yarmouth and Haddiscoe. Follow this road until you come to the junction with the A143 and turn left towards Great Yarmouth. A short distance on from here you cross the bridge over the river at St Olaves. Just after the bridge, you will see The Bell Inn on your right with the car park immediately after.

From Beccles – leave Beccles on the A146 and at the first roundabout turn onto the A143 towards Great Yarmouth. Continue to St Olaves and then once over the bridge, follow the directions as above.

Table of Waterside Pubs

	River	Pub Name	Location	Grid Ref.	Address
P1	Bure	Rising Sun	Coltishall Common	TG 276 198	28 Wroxham Road, Coltish
P2	Bure	Kings Head	Coltishall Common	TG 276 198	26 Wroxham Road, Coltish
P3	Bure	The King's Head	Wroxham	TG 303 182	Station Road, Hoveton, N
P4	Bure	The Swan Inn	Horning	TG 339 176	10 Lower Street, Horning,
P5	Bure	The Ferry Inn	Horning	TG 344 164	Ferry Road, Horning, NR1
P6	Bure	The Maltsters	Ranworth	TG 359 145	The Hill, Ranworth, NR13
P7	Bure	Acle Bridge Inn	Acle	TG 414 116	Acle Bridge, Old Road, N
P8	Bure	The Ferry Inn	Stokesby	TG 431 105	Riverfront, The Green, Sto
P9	Ant	Wayford Bridge Inn	Wayford Bridge	TG 348 249	Wayford Bridge, Stalham
P10	Ant	Sutton Staithe Hotel	Sutton	TG 382 237	Sutton, Stalham, Norfolk,
P11	Thurne	The Lion Inn	Thurne	TG 403 158	The Street, Thurne, NR29
P12	Thurne	The Norada	Potter Heigham	TG 420 185	Potter Heigham, NR29 5J
P13	Thurne	The Pleasure Boat	Hickling	TG 409 225	Staithe Road, Hickling, N
P14	Wensum	The Red Lion	Norwich	TG 239 090	79 Bishopgate, Norwich,
P15	Yare	The Rushcutters	Thorpe St Andrew	TG 263 089	46 Yarmouth Road, Thorp
P16	Yare	The Townhouse	Thorpe St Andrew	TG 256 084	18-22 Yarmouth Road, Th
P17	Yare	The Rivergarden	Thorpe St Andrew	TG 258 083	36 Yarmouth Road, Norw
P18	Yare	The Water's Edge	Kirby Bedon	TG 291 062	Woods End, Bramerton, I
P19	Yare	The Ferry House	Surlingham	TG 308 075	1 Ferry Road, Surlingham
P20	Yare	Coldham Hall	Surlingham	TG 324 071	Coldham Hall Carnser, S
P21	Yare	New Inn	Rockland	TG 328 046	12 New Inn Hill, Rockland
P22	Yare	Beauchamp Arms	Claxton	TG 350 044	Ferry Road, Langley, NR1
P23	Yare	The Reedcutter	Cantley	TG 382 034	Station Road, Cantley, N
P24	Yare	Lord Nelson	Reedham	TG 419 017	38 Riverside Road, Reedh
P25	Yare	Reedham Ferry Inn	Reedham	TG 407 015	Ferry Road, Reedham, N
P26	Yare	The Berney Arms	Berney Arms	TG 467 051	Berney Arms, Great Yarn
P27	Waveney	The Locks Inn	Geldeston	TM 390 908	Lock's Lane, Geldeston,
P28	Waveney	The Bell Inn	St Olaves	TM 457 994	Beccles Road, St Olaves
P29	Waveney	The Black Swan	Homersfield	TM 284 856	Church Lane, Homersfie

	Website	Contact No.	Accommodation
2 7EA	www.risingsuncoltishall.co.uk	01603 737440	N
2 7EA	www.kingsheadcoltishall.co.uk	01603 737426	B&B
NR12 8UR	www.greatbritishcarvery.co.uk/our-pubs/kings-head	01603 782429	N
AA	www.vintageinn.co.uk	01692 630316	B&B
	www.tfi-restaurants.co.uk	01692 630259	N
	www.ranworthmaltsters.co.uk	01603 270900	N
	www.aclebridge.co.uk	01493 750288	N
NR29 3EX	Find on FaceBook	01493 751096	N
LL	www.wayfordbridge.co.uk	01692 582414	Y
S	www.suttonstaithehotel.co.uk	01692 580244	Y
	www.thelionatthurne.com	01692 671806	N
	www.thenorada.co.uk	01692 670904	N
	www.thepleasureboatinn.com	01692 598870	N
	www.redlionnorwich.com	01603 620154	N
ew, NR7 0HE	www.chefandbrewer.com	01603 435403	N
ndrew, NR7 0EF	www.stonehouserestaurants.co.uk	01603 700600	N
olk, NR7 0EQ	www.therivergarden.co.uk	01603 703900	N
	www.watersedgewoodsend.co.uk	01508 538005	N
AR	www.surlinghamferry.co.uk	01508 538659	N
, NR14 7AN	www.coldhamhall.com	01508 538366	N
, NR14 7HP	Find on FaceBook	01508 538211	N
	www.beauchamparms.uk	01508 480247	N
	Find on FaceBook	01493 701099	B&B
3 3TE	www.lordnelsonpub.com	01493 701548	N
	www.reedhamferry.co.uk	01493 700429	Y
30 1SB	none	01493 700303	N
Suffolk NR34 0HS	Find on FaceBook and Instagram	01508 518414	N
E	www.bellinn-stolaves.co.uk	01493 488249	N
on, IP20 0ET	www.blackswanhomersfield.co.uk	01986 899050	Y

New Inn, Stokesby.

Waterside Pubs

River Bure

Rising Sun

OS Explorer OL40 Grid Ref: TG 276 198

Postcode: NR12 7EA

Address: 28 Wroxham Road, Coltishall

Telephone: 01603 737440

Website: www.risingsuncoltishall.co.uk

Launching: No

Waypoint: Yes

The Rising Sun is generally the first building you see as you approach Coltishall Common by river. The large, bright building looks beautiful and welcoming as you paddle towards it. Originally a granary and workers' cottages, the Rising Sun welcomes guests with traditional pub décor and fare.

Kings Head

OS Explorer OL40 Grid Ref: TG 276 198

Postcode: NR12 7EA

Address: 26 Wroxham Road, Coltishall

Telephone: 01603 737426

Website: www.kingsheadcoltishall.co.uk

Launching: No

Waypoint: Yes

Accommodation: B&B

A 17th-century inn only a short walk from the River Bure and close to Broads Authority 24 hour moorings. Traditionally styled, the Kings Head offers a variety of high quality meals that are available cooked freshly to order.

The King's Head

OS Explorer OL40 Grid Ref: TG 303 182

Postcode: NR12 8UR

Address: Station Road, Hoveton

Telephone: 01603 782429

Website: www.greeneking-pubs.co.uk/pubs/norfolk/kings-head-hotel/

Launching: No

Waypoint: Yes

A very pleasant pub specialising in a daily carvery with pub menu and specials. Easy access from the staithe at the end of the garden area.

The Swan Inn

Chain/group: Vintage Inns

OS Explorer OL40 Grid Ref: TG 339 176

Postcode: NR12 8AA

Address: 10 Lower Street, Horning

Telephone: 01692 630316

Website: www.vintageinn.co.uk/theswanhorning

Launching: Yes – public slipway and vertical drop-in close by

Waypoint: Yes

Accommodation: B&B

The Swan Inn is a very popular place to while away a few hours by the river watching the world go by on its boat. It has a large interior and also some outdoor tables that are right on the waterside. As a member of the Vintage Inns chain, you are guaranteed a wide choice of menu that should satisfy lighter and larger appetites alike. There is no car park on site, but the pay and display is only a few yards away.

The Ferry Inn, Horning

OS Explorer OL40 Grid Ref: TG 344 164

Postcode: NR12 8PS

Address: Ferry Road, Horning

Telephone: 01692 630259

Website: www.tfi-restaurants.co.uk

Launching: No

Waypoint: Yes

A spacious and welcoming carvery with plenty of riverside frontage and seating areas. Great selection of food and drink, even if you don't fancy a carvery. Games room, pool table and crazy golf available during summer months.

The Maltsters

OS Explore OL40 Grid Ref: TG 359 145

Postcode: NR13 6AB

Address: The Hill, Ranworth

Telephone: 01603 270900

Website: www.ranworthmaltsters.co.uk

Launching: No

Waypoint: Yes

The Maltsters delivers great food and drink with a beautiful view of the broad. Ample free parking opposite makes it not only a perfect place to pause but also a great launching point as well.

Acle Bridge Inn

OS Explorer OL40 Grid Ref: TG 414 116

Postcode: NR13 3AS

Address: Acle Bridge, Old Road

Telephone: 01493 750288

Website: www.aclebridge.co.uk

Launching: No

Waypoint: Yes

The Bridge Inn prides itself on being a family friendly pub that offers a warm welcome. There is a wide range of food and drink, along with plenty of facilities to keep the whole family entertained.

The Ferry Inn, Stokesby

OS Explorer OL40 Grid Ref: TG 431 105

Postcode: NR29 3EX

Address: Riverfront, The Green, Stokesby

Telephone: 01493 751096

Website: None

Launching: No, but mooring and staithe are very close.

Waypoint: Yes

The Ferry Inn has a large outdoor seating area and easy access to and from the river. A regularly changing menu and specials board keeps dining interesting, and the public car parking and easy launching nearby make Stokesby a great place to start and finish a paddle.

Rising Sun, Coltishall Common.

River Ant

Wayford Bridge Inn

OS Explorer OL40 Grid ref: TG 348 249

Postcode: NR12 9LL

Address: Wayford Bridge, Stalham

Telephone: 01692 582414

Website: www.wayfordbridge.co.uk

Launching: Yes

Waypoint: Yes

Accommodation: B&B

A very welcoming pub with superb food and locally sourced seafood. Located at the entry to the Dilham Canal, this is a great place to stop for a break when out paddling. Luxurious B&B accommodation is also available.

Sutton Staithe Hotel

OS Explorer OL40 Grid ref: TG 382 237

Postcode: NR12 9QS

Address: Sutton, Stalham,

Telephone: 01692 580244

Website: www.suttonstaithehotel.co.uk

Launching: Yes

Waypoint: Yes

Accommodation: B&B

Overlooking Sutton Staithe and the river Ant, the hotel has a great selection of food including a wide range of traditional mains and a very popular Sunday carvery. Fresh fish and daily specials are also available.

River Thurne

The Lion Inn

OS OL40 Grid Ref: TG 403 158

Postcode: NR29 3AP

Address: The Street, Thurne

Telephone: 01692 671806

Website: www.thelionatthurne.com

Launching: Yes – from staithe opposite

Waypoint: Yes

The Lion Inn is situated at the end of the dyke at Thurne, just off the river. It has a real charm and a very warm welcome serving well-priced food and drink. There is even an amusement arcade which is great if the kids have been paddling for a while and need a break.

The Norada

OS Explorer OL40 Grid Ref: TG 420 185

Postcode: NR29 5JD

Address: Potter Heigham

Telephone: 01692 670904

Website: www.thenorada.co.uk

Launching: No

Waypoint: Yes

Situated upstream of Potter Heigham bridge, the Broadshaven Tavern sits right on the water with plenty of outdoor seating and large grassy area. It's an ideal place to stop and watch the cruisers trying to navigate underneath the bridge. Moorings can be busy in peak season.

The Pleasure Boat Inn, Hickling.

Swan at Potter Heigham.

The Pleasure Boat Inn

OS Explorer OL40 Grid Ref: TG 409 225

Postcode: NR12 0YW

Address: Staithe Road, Hickling

Telephone: 01692 598870

Website: www.thepleasureboatinn.com

Launching: Yes

Waypoint: Yes

Situated at the far northern end of Hickling Broad, the Pleasure Boat can be a welcome sight if you have paddled all the way from the Thurne. A friendly place with a good selection of drink and well-priced hearty food – try the steak and ale pie.

River Wensum

The Red Lion

> **OS Explorer OL40 Grid Ref:** TG 239 090
> **Postcode:** NR1 4AA
> **Address:** 79 Bishopgate, Norwich
> **Telephone:** 01603 620154
> **Website:** www.redlionnorwich.com
> **Launching:** Yes
> **Waypoint:** Yes

The Red Lion is situated next to Bishop Bridge on the eastern side of the centre of Norwich city. Ideal for exploring the city stretch of the river or stopping for a break and re-fuel.

📷 *The Red Lion, Bishop Bridge.*

River Yare

The Rushcutters

> **Chain/group: Chef and Brewer**
> **OS OL40 Grid Ref:** TG 263 089
> **Postcode:** NR7 0HE
> **Address: 46 Yarmouth Road, Thorpe St Andrew**
> **Telephone: 01603 435403**
> **Website: www.chefandbrewer.com**
> **Launching: No**
> **Waypoint: Yes**

The 16th-century building houses a very welcoming pub. Well-delivered classic pub food and drink at good prices. The outdoor seating area extends right to the riverbank.

The Townhouse

> **Chain/group: Stonehouse Restaurants**
> **OS Explorer OL40 Grid Ref:** TG 256 084
> **Postcode:** NR7 0EF
> **Address: 18-22 Yarmouth Road,**
> **Thorpe St Andrew, Norwich**
> **Telephone: 01603 700600**
> **Website: www.stonehouserestaurants.co.uk**
> **Launching: No**

A great place to refuel when out on a paddle, the daily carvery at the Townhouse certainly doesn't disappoint. Great value, plenty of food and easily accessible from the Thorpe Loop.

The Rivergarden

OS Explorer OL40 Grid Ref: TG 258 083

Postcode: NR7 0EQ

Address: 36 Yarmouth Road, Norwich

Telephone: 01603 703900

Website: www.therivergarden.co.uk

Launching: No

Waypoint: Yes

A very pleasant place to pause for refreshment. Good food and drinks at reasonable prices with a large riverside seating area.

The Water's Edge

OS Explorer OL40 Grid Ref: TG 291 062

Postcode: NR14 7ED

Address: Woods End, Bramerton

Telephone: 01508 538005

Website: www.watersedgewoodsend.co.uk

Launching: No / difficult – parking restrictions

Waypoint: Yes

Thoroughly modernised with a great riverside seating and decking area incorporating BBQ.

The Woods End pub – now The Water's Edge.

The Ferry House

OS Explorer OL40 Grid Ref: TG 308 075

Postcode: NR14 7AR

Address: 1 Ferry Road, Surlingham

Telephone: 01508 538659

Website: www.surlinghamferry.co.uk

Launching: Yes

Waypoint: Yes

Possibly the warmest welcome for paddlers on the river, The Ferry House is a fantastic place from which to launch or simply stop while out on the Yare. With a new slipway currently being built, The Ferry House is perfect for paddlers. Great atmosphere, good food and drink, and situated right on the river.

Coldham Hall

OS Explorer OL40 Grid Ref: TG 324 071

Postcode: NR14 7AN

Address: Coldham Hall Carnser, Surlingham

Contact No: 01508 538366

Website: www.coldhamhall.com

Launching: Yes, vertical drop-in and small gravel beach

Waypoint: Yes

Beautifully decorated and very welcoming pub which serves a great selection of locally sourced food and drink. There are plenty of tables outside by the river for the summer time. Park and launch is allowed but please be sure to patronise the pub.

📷 *Beauchamp Arms.*

New Inn

OS Explorer OL40 Grid Ref: TG 328 046

Postcode: NR14 7HP

Address: 12 New Inn Hill, Rockland St Mary

Telephone: 01508 538211

Website: None

Launching: No

Waypoint: Yes

The New Inn sits at the start of the dyke that leads out to Rockland Broad. The car parking for the nearby launch site is almost immediately opposite the pub, so if you are out for a morning paddle this is ideally situated for a post-paddle drink or lunch. Good selection of drinks and a great menu. Outdoor seating also available overlooking the slipway.

Beauchamp Arms

OS Explorer OL40 Grid Ref: TG 350 044

Postcode: NR14 6DH

Address: Ferry Road, Langley

Telephone: 01508 480247

Website: www.beauchamparms.uk

Launching: Yes, vertical drop-in of around 50cm – free parking as long as paddlers use the pub for food or drink

Waypoint: Yes

A welcome place to pause for a rest as this stretch of river can be challenging in certain weather conditions. Long mooring makes for easy access. Plenty of outdoor seating.

The Reedcutter

📷 *Reedcutter.*

OS Explorer OL40 Grid Ref: TG 382 034

Postcode: NR13 3SH

Address: Station Road, Cantley

Telephone: 01493 701099

Website: None

Launching: from the staithe

Waypoint: Yes

Accommodation: B&B

The Reedcutter sits next to the Cantley Sugar Factory and has a newly upgraded staithe with excellent launching facilities. The pub has a friendly welcome with good selection of food and drink.

The Lord Nelson

OS Explorer OL40 Grid Ref: TG 419 017

Postcode: NR13 3TE

Address: 38 Riverside, Reedham

Telephone: 01493 700367

Website: www.lordnelsonpub.com

Launching: Yes, from staithe opposite

Waypoint: Yes

A popular and pleasant pub that represents a welcome stopping point for those paddling this stretch. A varied menu and plentiful supply of real ales, including from the local Humpty Dumpty Brewery, make this friendly pub an ideal place to pause, and it's only a few metres from the riverside.

Reedham Ferry Inn

OS Explorer OL40 Grid Ref: TG 407 015

Postcode: NR13 3HA

Address: Ferry Road, Reedham

Telephone: 01493 700429

Website: www.reedhamferry.co.uk

Launching: Yes

Waypoint: Yes

Reedham Ferry Inn is a wonderful place to either launch from, pause and refresh, or even use as a base from which to explore the Broads area, as the complex also incorporates the Reedham Ferry Touring Park and campsite.

📷 *Reedham Ferry Inn.*

Their motto 'We don't serve fast food, just good food as fast as we can,' certainly holds true, with a great selection of locally sourced fresh meat, fish and vegetables and, of course, their range of ales from both local and more well-known breweries is excellent. An extremely friendly welcome and a warm, inviting interior will almost keep you off the water.

The Berney Arms

OS Explorer OL40 Grid Ref: TG 467 051
Postcode: NR30 1SB
Address: Great Yarmouth
Telephone: 01493 700303
Website: None
Launching: No
Waypoint: Yes

Only accessible from the water or by foot, the Berney Arms has something of a mystique about it. You couldn't get a more unique, isolated and rural feel about a pub if you tried.

River Waveney

The Locks Inn

OS Explorer OL40 Grid Ref: TM 390 908
Postcode: NR34 0HS
Address: Lock's Lane, Geldeston
Telephone: 01508 518414
Website: None – Find on Facebook and Instagram
Launching: Yes – park in first car parking area before pub and walk down. Vertical drop-in of around 1m. Single ladder available.
Waypoint: Yes

Surely one of the hidden gems of the Broads, The Locks Inn has the warmest of welcomes combined with great choice of food and drink in a location most pubs can only dream of. The approach to the inn is down a fairly long, and very bumpy, track. Just before you get to the inn itself you come to an open car parking area. This is where the owners would like

The Berney Arms. Photo | Mark Rainsley.

Locks Inn, Geldeston.

paddlers to park if they wish to launch. Don't worry as the walk is only around 100 metres to the water. Launching is via a vertical drop-in of a little over one metre but there is a ladder built into the bank which makes it easier for kayaks. While there is no charge for launching at The Locks Inn, as a courtesy please be a patron while you are there – you'll find it difficult to resist and you won't regret it.

The Bell Inn

OS Explorer OL40 Grid Ref: TM 457 994
Postcode: NR31 9HE
Address: Beccles Road, St Olaves
Telephone: 01493 488249
Website: www.bellinn-stolaves.co.uk
Launching: Yes
Waypoint: Yes

The Bell is a great pub dating back to around 1520. It has a great feel and a warm welcome with some delicious food and a varied specials board. Their Sunday roasts are excellent and you'll need a paddle to work off one of their puddings. Parking for paddlers is permitted, but please go in and let them know who you are. They will ask that you please park in the car park but away from the pub itself. The river is only a few metres away.

The Black Swan

OS Explorer 230 Grid Ref: TM 284 856
Postcode: IP20 0ET
Address: Church Lane, Homersfield
Telephone: 01986 788204
Website: www.blackswanhomersfield.co.uk
Launching: Yes
Waypoint: Yes
Accommodation: Yes

Well known in paddling circles, the Black Swan is synonymous with canoeing the river Waveney. It sits only a few metres from the water and with its warm welcome, great selection of food and drink, and a campsite next door it really couldn't be better placed. It's almost worth planning a paddling trip just as an excuse to drop in for a visit, especially once you've tried something off their grill. Car parking is plentiful with areas on both sides of Homersfield Bridge; just watch out for the height restriction on the Wortwell side.

Table of Waterside Campsites

River	Campsite	Address
Bure	Salhouse Broad	Lower Street, Salhouse, NR13 6RX
Thurne	Willowcroft Camping & Caravan Site	Staithe Road, Repps with Bastwick, NR29 5JU
Thurne	Bureside Holiday Park	Boundary Farm, Oby, Great Yarmouth, NR29 3BW
Waveney	Outney Meadow Caravan Park	Bungay, Suffolk, NR35 1HG
Waveney	Waveney River Centre	Staithe Road, Burgh St Peter, NR34 0BT
Waveney	Three Rivers Camping	The Boat Shed, Geldeston, NR34 0LY
Waveney	The Black Swan	Church Lane, Homersfield, Harleston, IP20 0ET
Yare	Reedham Ferry Touring Park	Reedham, Norfolk, NR13 3HA
Yare	Whitlingham Broad Campsite	Whitlingham Lane, Norwich, NR14 8TR

Reedham Ferry Touring Park, River Yare.

Contact No.	Website	Camping	Caravans	Grid Ref.
01603 722775	www.salhousebroad.org.uk	Y	N	TG 318 149
01692 670380	www.willowcroft.net	Y	Y	TG 413 172
01493 369233	www.bureside.com	Y	Y	TG 404 151
01986 892338	www.outneymeadow.co.uk	Y	Y	TM 332 902
01502 677343	www.waveneyrivercentre.co.uk	Y	Y	TM 492 934
07948 552128	www.threeriverscamping.co.uk	Y	Y	TM 389 918
01986 899050	www.blackswanhomersfield.co.uk	Y	Y	TM 284 856
01493 700999	www.reedhamferry.co.uk	Y	Y	TG 406 015
07794 401591	www.whitlinghambroadcampsite.com	Y	N	TG 251 075

Outney Meadow Caravan Park, River Waveney.

Outney Meadow Campsite, River Waveney.

Waterside Campsites

River Thurne

Salhouse Broad Camping

> **OS Explorer OL40 Grid Ref:** TG318149
>
> **Postcode:** NR13 6RX
>
> **Address: Lower Street, Salhouse, Norfolk**
>
> **Telephone: 01603 722775**
>
> **Website: www.salhousebroad.org.uk**

A very basic campsite, Salhouse Broad does not offer luxury camping facilities. This location is ideally suited to an overnight stop off while exploring the area or as a base if you don't mind chemical toilets or a fairly long walk to the car park loos. No showers, but there is fresh drinking water available.

Willowcroft

> **OS Explorer OL40 Grid Ref:** TG 413 172
>
> **Postcode:** NR29 5JU
>
> **Address: Staithe Road, Repps with Bastwick, Potter Heigham, Norfolk**
>
> **Telephone: 01692 670380**
>
> **Website: www.willowcroft.net**

Willowcroft is a small, family run campsite close to Potter Heigham with easy access to the River Thurne. The two acre site features immaculately-kept grass pitches for tents, hardstandings with electric hook-up points for caravans and campers, and toilets and showers. So whether you are camping or bringing a caravan, Willowcroft is a great place to stay and explore the Broads.

Bureside

> **OS Explorer OL40 Grid Ref:** TG 404 151
>
> **Postcode:** NR29 3BW
>
> **Address: Bureside Holiday Park, Boundary Farm, Oby, Great Yarmouth**
>
> **Telephone: 01493 369233**
>
> **Website: www.buresideholidaypark.co.uk**

A working stud farm which caters for both tents and caravans, Bureside is ideal for paddlers as it also has its own slipway and dyke onto the Bure. It is situated close to the confluence of the Bure and Thurne making it perfectly situated for exploring as much of the northern Broads as you can manage. Facilities include toilets and showers, fishing lake, boat storage and even a swimming pool.

River Waveney

Outney Meadow

> OS Explorer OL40 Grid Ref: TM 332 902
>
> Postcode: NR35 1HG
>
> Address: Outney Meadow Caravan Park,
> Bungay
>
> Telephone: 01986 892338
>
> Website: www.outneymeadow.co.uk

📷 *Outney Meadow.*

Outney Meadow is a wonderful place for families to start their exploration of the Broads. From the moment you arrive, Colin and Mary Jane Hancey will give you the warmest of welcomes, and their site provides a wide range of well-kept grassy camping areas surrounded by trees and hedges that ensure your stay will be a peaceful one. The emphasis at Outney Meadow is very much low-key and informal, indeed it is a little like going to stay with your aunt and uncle who happen to own a camping and caravan site in the country, combined with a quick bit of time travel back to the 70s. On site are all the facilities you would expect and some of the camping pitches also have electric hook up points.

The campsite has access directly onto the River Waveney with excellent launching facilities and a small fleet of open canoes that you can hire if you don't have your own.

You can also launch from Outney Meadow even if you are not staying there. There is a small fee for open canoes and kayaks which also includes car parking.

Three Rivers Camping

> OS Explorer OL40 Grid Ref: TM389918
>
> Postcode: NR34 0LY
>
> Address: The Boat Shed, Station Road,
> Geldeston, Norfolk
>
> Telephone: 07948 552128
>
> Website: www.threeriverscamping.co.uk

Description: A family run site that welcomes tents, caravans and campervans. Three Rivers have a good amount of space and pitches with or without electric hook up points. They allocate you plenty of space so you're never pitched right on top of someone else and the

📷 *Waveney River Centre camping.*

river Waveney is right on your doorstep. Showers and toilets are available on site as well

Waveney River Centre

OS Explorer OL40 Grid Ref: TG 404 151

Postcode: NR34 0BT

Address: Waveney River Centre, Staithe Road, Burgh St Peter, Norfolk

Telephone: 01502 677343

Website: www.waveneyrivercentre.co.uk

The largest camping, touring or caravan and lodge holiday park on the Broads, the Waveney River Centre has all the facilities of a holiday camp with direct access onto the river, which makes it an ideal place to stay with a family wanting to explore the area.

The Black Swan – Homersfield

OS Explorer OL40 Grid Ref: TM 284 856

Postcode: IP20 0ET

Address: Church Lane, Homersfield, Harleston

Telephone: 01986 899050

Website: www.blackswanhomersfield.co.uk

A perfect location if you are planning a two-day trip along the Waveney. The Black Swan is well known to paddlers and the welcome there is warm. The camping area is between the pub and the river, only a short walk from the bridge.

River Yare

Reedham Ferry and The Archers Touring Park

OS Explorer OL40 Grid Ref: TG 406 015

Postcode: NR13 3HA

Address: Reedham Ferry Touring Park, Reedham Ferry Inn, Ferry Road, Norwich

Telephone: 01493 700999

Website: www.reedhamferry.co.uk

A warm welcome is assured at Reedham Ferry. The park is situated in a great setting and has a range of facilities. Not only do the owners openly welcome paddlers, but they also own and run the pub which has a wonderful atmosphere and some superb food and drink.

Whitlingham Broad Campsite

OS Explorer OL40 Grid Ref: TG 251 075

Postcode: NR14 8TR

Address: Whitlingham Lane,Norwich

Telephone: 07794 401591

Website: www.whitlinghambroadcampsite.com

The newest campsite close to the Broads, this spacious site lies close to Whitlingham Broad and the River Yare. An excellent landing stage makes getting off the river easy, however there is a portage of around 500m to reach the campsite. Facilities include good-sized pitches (fire pits and sturdy BBQs permitted), family friendly washrooms and a small shop.

Table of Canoe and Kayak Hire Centres

Location	Hire Centre Name	Address	Contact No.
Bungay	Outney Meadow Caravan Park	Outney Meadow, Bungay, Suffolk, NR35 1HG	01986 892338
Burgh St Peter	Waveney River Centre	Burgh St Peter, Suffolk, NR34 0BT	01502 677343
Geldeston	Rowan Craft	Wherry Dyke, Geldeston, Beccles, NR34 0LY	01508 518208
Hickling	Whispering Reeds Boats Ltd.	Staithe Road, Hickling, Norwich, NR12 0YW	01692 598314
Martham	Martham Boats	Valley Works, Cess Road, Martham, NR29 4RF	01493 740249
Salhouse	Salhouse Broad	Car park: Lower Street, Salhouse, NR13 6RX	01603 722775 07795 145475
Sutton Staithe	Sutton Staithe Boatyard	Sutton Staithe, Sutton, Norfolk, NR12 9QS	01692 518653
Wayford Bridge	Bank Boats	Wayford Bridge, Norfolk, NR12 9LN	01692 582457
Wroxham	Barnes Brinkcraft	Riverside Road, Wroxham, NR12 8UD	01603 782625
NON-HIRE NETWORK			
Potter Heigham	Herbert Woods	Broads Haven, Potter Heigham, NR29 5JF	0800 1444472
Whitlingham Broad	Whitlingham Outdoor Education Centre	Whitlingham Lane, Trowse, Norwich, NR14 8TR	01603 632307
Wroxham	Wroxham Boat Hire	The Broads Centre, Riverside Road, NR12 8UD	01603 783051
Norwich	Pub and Paddle	N/A	07886 080875

Grid Ref.	Website / email	Charges
TM 333 904	Web: www.outneymeadow.co.uk Email: info@outneymeadow.co.uk	£25 half day £40 all day 9-5pm
TM 492 934	Web: www.waveneyrivercentre.co.uk Email: info@waveneyrivercentre.co.uk	From £35 for a half day
TM 389 917	Web: www.rowancraft.co.uk Email: marina@rowancraft.co.uk	
TG 409 225	Web: www.whisperingreeds.net Email: info@whisperingreeds.net	
TG 438 191	Web: www.marthamboats.com Email: info@marthamboats.com	£25 for 3hr from £35 for 6hr
TG 139 150	Web: www.salhousebroad.org.uk Email: tbaker@salhousebroad.org.uk	1 hr £14 / 3 hr £30 / 6 hr £48 Kayaks also available. Open from April - October 1100 - 1800
TG 382 237	Web: www.suttonstaitheboatyard.co.uk Email: info@suttonstaitheboatyard.co.uk	3 hr £25 / 6 hr £40 Sit on tops also available.
TG 347 247	Web: www.bankboats.co.uk Email: urwin@clara.net	3 hr £25 / 6 hr £40 Kayak hire also available.
TG 304 197	Web: www.barnesbrinkcraft.co.uk Email: bookings@barnesbrinkcraft.co.uk	3 hr £30-39 / 6 hr £45 - £55 low / high season
TG 419 184	Web: www.herbertwoods.co.uk Email: enquiries@herbertwoods.co.uk	4 hr £35 / 7 hr £50
TG 253 077	Web: www.whitlinghamadventure.org.uk Email:whitlingham@educatorsolutions.org.uk	From £12 per hour. Range of sit on tops, kayaks and canoes available. Hire available from April to October.
TG 304 179	Web: www.wroxhamboathire.co.uk Email: bookings@.wroxhamboathire.co.uk	
N/A	Web: www.pubandpaddle.com Email: info@pubandpaddle.com	Wooden canoes built locally Trips arranged direct

Distance Charts

Bure (km)	Horstead Mill	Coltishall Common	Belaugh	Hoveton Riverside Park	Wroxham Broad	Salhouse Broad	Hoveton Little Broad	Horning	Horning Ferry	Malthouse Broad	Bure / Ant Junction	South Walsham Broad	Bure / Thurne Junction	Upton Dyke	The Bridge Inn, Acle	Stokesby	Gt. Yarmouth Yacht Stn.	Bure / Yare Junction
Horstead Mill		1.5	3.5	9.2	12.7	14.4	17.1	17.9	19.3	23.3	24.0	26.5	27.3	30.5	32.0	35.3	49.8	50.3
Coltishall Common	1.5		2.0	7.7	11.2	12.9	15.6	16.4	17.8	21.8	22.5	25.0	25.8	29.0	30.5	33.8	48.3	58.8
Belaugh	3.5	2.0		5.7	9.2	10.9	13.6	14.4	15.8	19.8	20.5	23.0	23.8	27.0	28.5	31.8	46.3	46.8
Hoveton Riverside Park	9.2	7.7	5.7		3.5	5.2	7.9	8.7	10.1	14.1	14.8	17.3	18.1	21.3	22.8	26.1	40.6	41.1
Wroxham Broad	12.7	11.2	9.2	3.5		2.1	4.8	5.6	7.0	11.0	11.7	14.2	15.0	18.2	19.7	23.0	37.5	38.0
Salhouse Broad	14.4	12.9	10.9	5.2	2.1		2.7	3.5	4.9	8.9	9.6	12.1	12.9	16.1	17.6	20.9	35.4	35.9
Hoveton Little Broad	17.1	15.6	13.6	7.9	4.8	2.7		0.8	2.2	6.2	6.9	12.4	13.2	16.4	17.9	21.2	35.7	36.2
Horning	19.3	16.4	14.4	8.7	5.6	3.5	0.8		1.4	5.4	6.1	8.6	9.4	12.6	14.1	17.4	31.9	32.4
Horning Ferry	19.3	17.8	15.8	10.1	7.0	4.9	2.2	1.4		4.0	4.7	7.2	8.0	11.2	12.7	16.0	30.5	31.0
Malthouse Broad	23.3	21.8	19.8	14.1	11.0	8.9	6.2	5.4	4.0		3.1	5.6	6.4	9.6	11.1	14.4	28.9	29.4
Bure / Ant Junction	24.0	22.5	20.5	14.8	11.7	9.6	6.9	6.1	4.7	3.1		2.5	3.3	6.5	8.0	11.3	25.8	26.3
South Walsham Broad	26.5	25.0	23.0	17.3	14.2	12.1	12.4	8.6	7.2	5.6	2.5		4.8	8.0	9.5	12.8	27.3	27.8
Bure / Thurne Junction	27.3	25.8	23.8	18.1	15.0	12.9	13.2	9.4	8.0	6.4	3.3	4.8		3.2	4.7	8.0	22.5	23.0
Upton Dyke	30.5	29.0	27.0	21.3	18.2	16.1	16.4	12.6	11.2	9.6	6.5	8.0	3.2		2.9	6.2	20.7	21.2
The Bridge Inn, Acle	32.0	30.5	28.5	22.8	19.7	17.6	17.9	14.1	12.7	11.1	8.0	9.5	4.7	2.9		3.3	17.8	18.3
Stokesby	35.3	33.8	31.8	26.1	23.0	20.9	21.2	17.4	16.0	14.4	11.3	12.8	8.0	6.2	3.3		14.5	15.0
Gt. Yarmouth Yacht Stn.	49.8	48.3	46.3	40.6	37.5	35.4	35.7	31.9	30.5	28.9	25.8	27.3	22.5	20.7	17.8	14.5		0.5
Bure / Yare Junction	50.3	58.8	46.8	41.1	38.0	35.9	36.2	32.4	31.0	29.4	26.3	27.8	23.0	21.2	18.3	15.0	0.5	

Ant (km)

	Honing Lock	Dilham Staithe	Wayford Bridge	Stalham Staithe	Sutton Staithe	Barton Turf	Gay's Staithe	Neatishead Staithe	Irstead Moorings	How Hill	Ludham Bridge	Ant / Bure Junction
Honing Lock		5.4	3.8	8.2	8.3	7.7	9.6	10.2	9.5	11.5	14.9	16.4
Dilham Staithe	5.4		2.0	6.4	6.5	5.9	7.8	8.4	7.7	9.7	13.1	14.6
Wayford Bridge	3.8	2.0		4.4	4.5	3.9	5.8	6.4	5.7	7.7	11.4	12.6
Stalham Staithe	8.2	6.4	4.4		2.5	3.3	5.2	5.8	5.1	7.1	10.5	12.0
Sutton Staithe	8.3	6.5	4.5	2.5		3.4	5.3	5.9	5.2	7.2	10.6	12.1
Barton Turf	7.7	5.9	3.9	3.3	3.4		2.4	3.0	2.5	2.5	7.9	9.4
Gay's Staithe	9.6	7.8	5.8	5.2	5.3	2.4		0.6	2.1	4.1	7.5	9.0
Neatishead Staithe	10.2	8.4	6.4	5.8	5.9	3.0	0.6		2.7	4.7	8.1	9.6
How Hill	11.5	9.7	7.7	7.1	7.2	2.5	4.1	4.7	2.0		3.4	4.9
Ludham Bridge	14.9	13.1	11.4	10.5	10.6	7.9	7.5	8.1	5.4	3.4		1.5
Ant / Bure Junction	16.4	14.6	12.6	12.0	12.1	9.4	9.0	9.6	6.9	4.9	1.5	

Thurne (km)

	Horsey Mill	Hickling	Catfield Common	Martham	West Somerton*	Potter Heigham Bridge	Repps with Bastwick	Ludham Staithe	Thurne Dyke	Thurne / Bure Junction
Horsey Mill		6.0	6.5	5.1	11.3	7.1	8.6	11.4	11.8	12.8
Hickling	6.0		2.1	5.1	11.3	7.1	8.6	11.4	11.8	12.8
Catfield Common	6.5	2.1		5.6	8.8	7.6	8.8	11.6	12.0	13.0
Martham	5.1	5.1	5.6		3.8	2.0	3.2	6.0	6.4	7.4
West Somerton*	11.3	11.3	8.8	3.8		5.8	7.0	9.8	10.2	11.2
Potter Heigham Bridge	7.1	7.1	7.6	2.0	5.8		1.2	4.0	4.4	5.4
Repps with Bastwick	8.6	8.6	8.8	3.2	7.0	1.2		2.8	3.2	4.2
Ludham Staithe	11.4	11.4	11.6	6.0	9.8	4.0	2.8		3.0	4.0
Thurne Dyke	11.8	11.8	12.0	6.4	10.2	4.4	3.2	3.0		0.9
Thurne / Bure Junction	12.8	12.8	13.0	7.4	11.2	5.4	4.2	4.0	0.9	

*Please note: no launching at West Somerton – parishioners only

Yare (km)

	New Mills	Friars Quay, Norwich	Red Lion Inn	Whitlingham Broad	Cary's Meadow	Thorpe St Andrew	Whitlingham Woods	Water's Edge	Bramerton Common	The Ferry House	Coldham Hall	Rockland Broad	Beauchamp Arms	Langley Dyke	Cantley Staithe	Yare / Chet Conf.	Reedham Ferry	Reedham	Yare / New Cut Conf.	Berney Arms	Yare / Waveney Conf.	Yare / Bure Conf.
New Mills		0.5	1.8	4.5	5	5.5	6.7	10.5	11	13.5	17	21	21	24.5	25.6	29.6	30.4	31.9	32.7	39.5	39.7	45.7
Friars Quay, Norwich	0.5		1.3	4.0	4.5	5.0	6.2	10.0	10.5	13.0	16.5	20.5	20.5	24.0	25.1	29.1	29.9	31.4	32.2	39.0	39.2	45.2
Red Lion Inn	1.8	1.3		2.8																		
Whitlingham Broad	4.5	4.0	2.8		0.5	1.0	2.2	6.0	6.5	9.0	12.5	16.5	16.5	20.0	21.1	25.1	25.9	27.4	28.2	35.0	35.2	41.2
Cary's Meadow	5.0	4.5	3.3	0.5		0.5	1.7	5.3	5.8	8.8	11.8	15.8	15.8	19.3	20.4	24.4	25.2	26.7	27.5	34.3	34.5	40.5
Thorpe St Andrew	5.5	5.0	3.8	1.0	0.5		1.2	4.9	5.4	7.9	11.4	15.4	15.4	18.9	20.0	24.0	24.8	26.3	27.1	33.9	34.1	40.1
Whitlingham Woods	6.7	6.2	5.0	2.2	1.7	1.2		3.6	4.1	6.6	10.1	14.1	14.1	17.6	18.7	22.7	23.5	25.0	25.8	32.6	32.8	38.8
Water's Edge	10.5	10.0	8.6	6.0	5.3	4.9	3.6		0.5	3.0	6.5	10.5	10.5	14.0	15.1	19.1	19.9	21.4	22.2	29.0	29.2	35.2
Bramerton Common	11.0	10.5	9.1	6.5	5.8	5.4	4.1	0.5		2.5	6.0	10.0	10.0	13.5	14.6	18.6	19.4	20.9	21.7	28.5	28.7	34.7
The Ferry House	13.5	13.0	11.6	9.0	8.8	7.9	6.6	3.0	2.5		3.5	7.5	7.5	11.0	12.1	16.1	16.9	18.4	19.2	26.0	26.2	32.2
Coldham Hall	17.0	16.5	15.1	12.5	11.8	11.4	10.1	6.5	6.0	3.5		4.0	4.0	7.5	8.6	12.6	13.4	14.8	15.7	22.5	22.7	28.7
Rockland Broad	21.0	20.5	19.1	16.5	15.8	15.4	14.1	10.5	10.0	7.5	4.0		3.0	6.5	7.6	11.6	12.4	13.8	14.7	21.5	21.7	27.7
Beauchamp Arms	21.0	20.5	19.1	16.5	15.8	15.4	14.1	10.5	10.0	7.5	4.0	3.0		3.5	4.6	8.6	9.4	10.8	11.7	18.5	18.7	24.7
Langley Dyke	24.5	24.0	22.6	20.0	19.3	18.9	17.6	14.0	13.5	11.0	7.5	6.5	3.5		2.0	6.0	6.8	8.3	9.1	15.9	16.1	22.1
Cantley Staithe	25.6	25.1	23.7	21.1	20.4	20.0	18.7	15.1	14.6	12.1	8.6	7.6	4.6	2.0		4.0.	4.8	6.3	7.1	13.9	14.1	20.1
Yare / Chet Conf.	29.6	29.1	27.7	25.1	24.4	24.0	22.7	19.1	18.6	16.1	12.6	11.6	8.6	6.0	4.0		0.8	2.3	3.1	9.9	10.1	16.1
Reedham Ferry	30.4	29.9	28.5	25.9	25.2	24.8	23.5	19.9	19.4	16.9	13.4	12.4	9.4	6.8	4.8	0.8		1.5	2.3	9.1	9.3	15.3
Reedham	31.9	31.4	30.0	27.4	26.7	26.3	25.0	21.4	20.9	18.4	14.8	13.8	10.8	8.3	6.3	2.3	1.5		0.8	7.6	7.8	13.8
Yare / New Cut Conf.	32.7	32.2	30.8	28.2	27.5	27.1	25.8	22.2	21.7	19.2	15.7	14.7	11.7	9.1	7.1	3.1	2.3	8.0		6.8	7.0	13.0
Berney Arms	39.5	39.0	37.6	35.0	34.3	33.9	32.6	29.0	28.5	26.0	22.5	21.5	18.5	15.9	13.9	9.9	9.1	7.6	6.8		0.2	6.2
Yare / Waveney Conf.	39.7	39.2	37.8	35.2	34.5	34.1	32.8	29.2	28.7	26.2	22.7	21.7	18.7	16.1	14.1	10.1	9.3	7.8	7.0	0.2		6.0
Yare / Bure Conf.	45.7	45.2	43.8	41.2	40.5	40.1	38.8	35.2	34.7	32.2	28.7	27.7	24.7	22.1	20.1	16.1	15.3	13.8	13.0	6.2	6.0	

If joining Waveney via New Cut, add 4kms

Chet (km)

	Loddon Launching Point	Pyes Mill	Chet / Yare Confluence
Loddon Launching Point		0.5	5.5
Pyes Mill	0.5		5.0
Chet / Yare Confluence	5.5	5.0	

Waveney (km)

	Shotford Bridge	Homersfield Bridge	Bungay Castle Wall	Outney Meadow	Bungay Sluice	Wainford Bridge	Ellingham Mill	Locks Inn Geldeston	Rowan Craft Geldeston	Beccles Quay	Waveney River Centre	Oulton Broad	Somerleyton Staithe	Waveney / New Cut Conf	St Olaves	Burgh Castle	Waveney / Yare Conf.	Waveney / Bure Conf.
Shotford Bridge		7.9	16.9	21.9	22.9	23.9	25.9	29.4	31.2	34.6	45.6	50.1	51.8	54.8	55.3	62.8	64.0	70.0
Homersfield Bridge	7.9		9.0	14.0	15.0	16.0	18.0	21.5	23.3	26.7	37.7	42.2	43.9	46.9	47.4	54.9	56.1	62.1
Bungay Castle Wall	16.9	9.0		5.0	6.0	7.0	9.0	12.5	14.3	17.7	28.7	33.2	34.9	37.9	38.4	45.9	47.1	53.1
Outney Meadow	21.9	14.0	5.0		1.0	2.0	4.0	7.5	9.3	12.7	23.7	28.2	29.9	32.9	33.4	40.9	42.1	48.1
Bungay Sluice	22.9	15.0	6.0	1.0		1.0	3.0	6.5	8.3	11.7	22.7	27.2	28.9	31.9	32.4	39.9	41.1	47.1
Wainford Bridge	23.9	6.0	7.0	2.0	1.0		2.0	5.5	7.3	10.7	21.7	26.2	27.9	30.9	31.4	38.9	40.1	46.1
Ellingham Mill	25.9	18.0	9.0	4.0	3.0	2.0		3.5	5.3	8.7	19.7	24.2	25.9	28.9	29.4	36.9	38.1	44.1
Locks Inn Geldeston	29.4	21.5	12.5	7.5	6.5	5.5	3.5		1.8	5.2	16.2	20.7	22.4	25.4	25.9	33.4	34.6	40.6
Rowan Craft Geldeston	31.2	23.3	14.3	9.3	8.3	7.3	5.3	1.8		5.0	16.0	20.5	22.2	25.2	25.7	33.2	34.4	40.4
Beccles Quay	34.6	26.7	17.7	12.7	11.7	10.7	8.7	5.2	5.0		11.0	15.5	17.2	20.2	20.7	28.2	29.4	35.4
Waveney River Centre	45.6	37.7	28.7	23.7	22.7	21.7	19.7	16.2	16.0	11.0		4.5	6.2	9.2	9.7	17.2	18.4	24.4
Oulton Broad	50.1	42.2	33.2	28.2	27.2	26.2	24.2	20.7	20.5	15.5	4.5		8.0	11.0	11.5	19.2	20.2	26.2
Somerleyton Staithe	51.8	43.9	34.9	29.9	28.9	27.9	25.9	22.4	22.4	17.2	6.2	8.0		3.0	3.5	18.5	12.2	18.2
Waveney / New Cut Conf.	54.8	46.9	37.9	32.9	31.9	30.9	28.9	25.4	25.2	20.2	9.2	11.0	3.0		0.5	8.0	9.2	15.2
St Olaves	55.3	47.4	38.4	33.4	32.4	31.4	29.4	25.9	25.7	20.7	9.7	11.5	3.5	0.5		7.5	8.7	14.7
Burgh Castle	62.8	54.9	45.9	40.9	39.9	39.9	36.9	33.4	33.2	28.8	17.2	19.0	11.0	8.0	7.5		1.2	7.2
Waveney / Yare Conf.	64.0	56.1	47.1	42.1	41.1	40.1	38.1	34.6	34.4	29.4	18.4	20.2	12.2	9.2	8.7	1.2		6.0
Waveney / Bure Conf.	70.0	62.1	53.1	48.1	47.1	46.1	44.1	40.6	40.4	35.4	24.4	26.2	18.2	15.2	14.7	7.2	6.0	

Sailboat on Meadow Dyke, River Thurne.

High Tide Times around The Broads

For the approximate time of High Water in the locations listed, **add** the times in the 2nd column to the time of High Water at Gorleston.

Location	High Water +
Lowestoft / Lake Lothing	35 min
Yarmouth Yacht Station	1 hour
Burgh Castle	1 hour
Reedham	2 hours 30 mins
St Olaves	2 hours 30 mins
Acle Bridge	3 hours 30 mins
Loddon	3 hours 30 mins
Oulton Broad	4 hours
Horning	4 hours
Beccles	4 hours
Potter Heigham	4 hours
Brundall	4 hours
Ludham Bridge	4 hours
Norwich	4 hours 30 mins
Wroxham	4 hours 30 mins
Coltishall	5 hours
Stalham	5 hours

Hickling Broad.

Appendix - Broads Authority Canoe Trails

SALHOUSE BROAD CANOE TRAILS

Salhouse Broad, Lower Street, Salhouse NR13 6RX   01603 722775 or 07795 145475

www.salhousebroad.org.uk

1hr – Explore Salhouse Broad

3hrs – Salhouse Broad to Horning and return

6hrs – Salhouse Broad to Ranworth and return

BUNGAY LOOP CANOE TRAIL

Outney Meadow Caravan Park,Outney Meadow, Bungay NR35 1HG   01986 892338

www.outneymeadow.co.uk

3hrs – Bungay loop and return

GELDESTON CANOE TRAILS

Rowan Craft, Wherry Dyke, Geldeston, Beccles NR34 0LY   01508 518208

www.rowancraft.com

1 hour – Geldeston village to Geldeston Lock and return

3–6hrs – Geldeston to Beccles and return

WAYFORD BRIDGE CANOE TRAILS

Bank Boats, Wayford Bridge NR12 9LN

01692 582457

www.bankboats.co.uk

3hrs – North Walsham and Dilham Canal and return

3hrs – Wayford Bridge to Stalham and return

3hrs – Wayford Bridge to Sutton and return

3hrs – Wayford Bridge to Neatishead and return

6hrs – Wayford Bridge to How Hill and return

SUTTON STAITHE CANOE TRAILS

Sutton Staithe Boatyard, Sutton Staithe, Sutton NR12 9QS   01692 581653

www.suttonstaitheboatyard.co.uk

3hrs – Sutton Staithe to Stalham and return

3hrs – Sutton Staithe to Wayford Bridge and return

3hrs – Sutton Staithe to Neatishead and return

6hrs – Sutton Staithe to How Hill and return

The following guides were reproduced with the kind permission of the Broads Authority.

BUNGAY LOOP CANOE TRAIL

Broads Authority
The Broads - a member of the
National Park family

Outney Meadow Caravan Park, Outney Meadow,
Bungay NR35 1HG 01986 892338
www.outneymeadow.co.uk

The canoe hire network may make a small charge or ask for a donation for launching your own canoe. This includes use of car parks and toilets.

Here is a suggested route, whether you are paddling your own canoe or hiring one. No experience is necessary and the route is suitable for families with children. Timing is approximate and you'll have plenty of time for breaks. Please make sure you take all you need in the way of food and drink on this route as there are no 'services'. You can make up for this before or after your paddle with a visit to Bungay which has plenty of shops and places for refreshment. You can also visit ruined **Bungay Castle**. Please check opening times and other details. **www.enjoythebroads.com**

3 hours – Bungay loop and return

- Part of the joy of this route is that it's entirely through open marshland with very little intruding on the lovely views of open water, riverbanks, willows and open skies.
- The water here is very clear – you can peer into it to spot bream or pike. Look out too for freshwater mussels and water birds including swans, herons and kingfishers. Owls may be around in the late afternoon or early evening. Otters live in the river and you may be lucky enough to see one. During the summer the whole area is full of butterflies, dragonflies and damselflies, especially the banded demoiselle damselfly and the beautiful demoiselle damselfly. You should see yellow water lilies too.
- Starting from the **caravan park**, paddle upstream (left). Where the river forks, take the channel on the right. The left hand channel is called the **Old River**. It's the original course of the **River Waveney** before the newer channel was dug to supply water to a mill.
- Shortly afterwards there's a narrow channel to the right. Stay on the main river and go under the small footbridge.

- The loop goes past **Baldry's Mill**. George Baldry was a local folk hero whose life story is told in *The Rabbit Skin Cap*, edited by Lilias Rider Haggard. Here stood the Mill House where George had his boats which he used to hire, and the workshops where he strove for the secret of perpetual motion. Lilias and her father, Henry Rider Haggard, author of many Victorian adventure stories, are buried at St Mary's Church, Ditchingham.
- **Outney Common** owners all hold one or more of the 300 shares known as 'goings'. A going will allow half a cow or a sheep to graze the meadow, so if you have a cow to graze you need at least two goings. The meadow was also used as a site for horse racing for 200 years.
- The common contains a large deposit of sands and gravel known as '**The Hards**' since at least the 1880s. The lower lying river valley areas either side are known as '**The Lows**'. Cattle graze on The Lows in summer and The Hards in winter when the marshy Lows would be too wet for them.
- The common also has a **golf course** so do watch out for golf balls heading for the river.
- **Bath Hills** are steeped in history. In Georgian times a cold spring existed there and Bungay was a famous spa town, attracting visitors from far and wide who came to take the waters. The hills are south facing – there were vineyards on them for centuries, even going back to Roman times. Roger Bigod (whose family built Bungay Castle) had extensive vineyards here in 1240.
- Across the common on a clear day you have a really good view of the Bungay skyline.
- There is usually plenty of clear water washing over the gravel – you can see the bottom of the river easily. You can also see the workings of the quarry. The Waveney was one of the southernmost valleys created in the last ice age, and the area is widely used for quarrying sand and shingle deposited at the time of the ice age.
- The **road bridge** marks the end of the route. The Waveney flows from Lopham Fen just west of Diss and out to sea at Great Yarmouth. During the summer it can be very shallow further upstream from the road bridge.
- If you have any spare time on return to the hire centre have a paddle the other way towards Beccles.

If you have any problems please contact your Canoe Hire Centre. You can also contact Broads Control on 01603 756056, staffed daily 9am-6pm from April to October and 9am-5pm during the winter. If the incident is more serious please call 999 or 112 and ask for the appropriate emergency service, which may be the coastguard.

BUNGAY LOOP CANOE TRAIL

Broads Authority
The Broads - a member of the National Park family

Please make sure you take all you need in the way of food and drink on this route as there are no 'services'.

KEY
- Canoe hire
- Places to get in and out

3 hours *(approx. 7km/4 miles)*
Bungay loop and return

Starting from the caravan park, paddle upstream (left). Where the river forks, take the channel on the right. The left hand channel is called the Old River. It's the original course of the River Waveney before the newer channel was dug to supply water to a mill. Shortly afterwards there's a narrow channel to the right. Stay on the main river and go under the small footbridge. Follow the Bungay loop all the way round to the road bridge which marks the end of the route.

These maps are for illustrative purposes only and are not drawn to scale.

Contains Ordnance Survey data © Crown copyright and database right 2013

Outney Meadow Caravan Park, Outney Meadow, Bungay NR35 1HG
01986 892338
www.outneymeadow.co.uk

Here are some suggestions for your route, whether you are paddling your own canoe or hiring one. No experience is necessary and routes are suitable for families with children. Times are approximate.

Paler blue areas of water are not open to any boats.

If you have any problems please contact your Canoe Hire Centre. You can also contact Broads Control on 01603 756056, staffed daily 9am–6pm from April to October and 9am–5pm during the winter. If the incident is more serious please call 999 or 112 and ask for the appropriate emergency service, which may be the coastguard.

Norwich
Lowestoft
B1332

Baldry's Mill

Sandy Corner

Old River

R. Waveney

The Lows

Outney Common

Hard Dyke

Canoe Hire
Outney Meadow
Caravan Park
01986 892338

3 HOUR TRAIL ENDS HERE

The Hards

golf course

R. Waveney

The Lows

Free Lane

Bath Hills plantation

N

Bath Hills Road

i WC
P
A143

BUNGAY

Bungay Castle

2 Mers Seas Zeeën
INTERREG IVA
NEDERLAND

"Investing in your future"
Crossborder cooperation programme
2007-2013 Part-financed by the European Union
(European Regional Development Fund)

STEP

GELDESTON CANOE TRAILS

Broads Authority
The Broads - a member of the
National Park family

Rowan Craft, Wherry Dyke, Geldeston,
Beccles NR34 0LY 01508 518208
www.rowancraft.com

The canoe hire centre makes a charge for launching your own canoe. This includes use of car park and toilets.

Here are some suggestions for your route, whether you are paddling your own canoe or hiring one. No experience is necessary and routes are suitable for families with children. Times are approximate and allow for a short stop on the 1 hour trail and breaks on the 6 hour trail. Please check opening times and other details for places mentioned below.
www.enjoythebroads.com

1 hour – Geldeston village to Geldeston Lock and return

- Owls and deer live around the **boatyard**. The good water quality produces a wealth of fish including bream, roach, perch and pike. Otters are back living in the wild on the river and have been sighted regularly within the yard for the first time in many years. Look out along the way for kingfishers and nesting swans too in spring.
- Paddle down the **dyke** and at the end turn right on to the **River Waveney**.
- The **Locks Inn** is one of the oldest pubs in the Broads, with a fascinating history. If you stop at the lock you can read a bit about the area or to find out more in advance of your visit watch *Memories of Geldeston* on **www.enjoythebroads.com** or listen to *Walk around Geldeston Lock* on **www.broads-authority.gov.uk**
- In 1670 an Act of Parliament was passed to improve the navigation upstream of Beccles and three locks were built, at Geldeston, Ellingham and Wainford. This made it possible for sailing wherries laden with cargo to travel to Bungay, with its brewing and malting industries. Ellingham and Geldeston were also railway stations on the now dismantled Waveney Valley Line, on the north side of the river, opened in the early 1860s.
- If you've no time to linger at the Locks, try the **Wherry Inn** at Geldeston village for refreshment before or after your paddle.

3-6 hours – Geldeston to Beccles and return

- Keener paddlers will comfortably make it to Beccles and back in 3 hours.
- With 6 hours you can go at a more leisurely pace with time for some breaks.
- This is a lovely, tranquil stretch of the river with few large boats.
- Paddle down the dyke and at the end turn left on to the River Waveney.
- As you pass **Dunburgh Hill** on the left (a hill in relative terms only!), look at the large area of reed on your right – marsh harriers nest there in the reed close to the ground.
- Continue past **Barsham Marshes** on your right. There is evidence here of a Bronze Age river crossing or ferry point.
- Towards Beccles the large buildings on the right hand side are part of the old industrial area of the town which included maltings, glassworks and tanneries.
- **Beccles Lido** is close to the river if you fancy a dip to cool off and the **information centre** down at the **quay** will help you with all the local information you may need.
- **Beccles Church** is unusual as its tower is separate from the rest of the building. The tower has three clock faces but not a fourth. The side without a clock is the one facing Norfolk – a reminder that the river is the boundary between Norfolk and Suffolk. You can sometimes climb the tower for fantastic views across the marshes. If that's not possible the view from ground level is lovely too.
- **Beccles Museum** will tell you all about the history of the town and is located in the beautiful Sir John Leman House which dates originally from the 16th century.
- Beccles is a real market town with a market on Fridays in New Market Place. It's good for shopping and has places for all kinds of refreshments.
- If you go through Beccles and under the **Old** and **New Bridges**, you can moor up and have a walk on **Beccles Marshes** to see the site of recent archaeological explorations which have uncovered remains dating from 75 BC.

If you have any problems please contact your Canoe Hire Centre. You can also contact Broads Control on 01603 756056, staffed daily 9am-6pm from April to October and 9am-5pm during the winter. If the incident is more serious please call 999 or 112 and ask for the appropriate emergency service, which may be the coastguard.

GELDESTON CANOE TRAILS

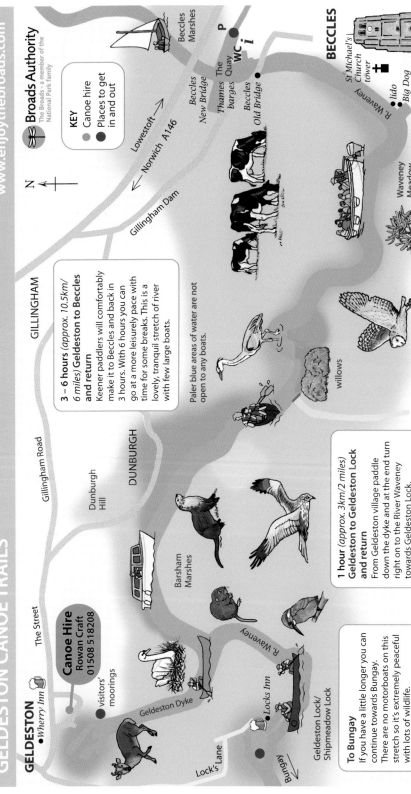

GELDESTON

The Street

Canoe Hire
Rowan Craft
01508 518208

visitors' moorings

Geldeston Dyke

Geldeston Lock/ Shipmeadow Lock

Lock's Lane

To Bungay
Locks Inn

R. Waveney

GILLINGHAM

Gillingham Road

Dunburgh Hill

DUNBURGH

Barsham Marshes

Gillingham Dam

Norwich A146

Lowestoft

Broads Authority
The Broads - a member of the National Park family

KEY
- Canoe hire
- Places to get in and out

N

Beccles Marshes

Beccles New Bridge

The Quay

Beccles Old Bridge

Thames barges

P

WC

i

BECCLES

St Michael's Church tower

R. Waveney

lido

Big Dog Ferry

Waveney Meadow

Beccles Museum

willows

3 – 6 hours (approx. 10.5km/6 miles) Geldeston to Beccles and return
Keener paddlers will comfortably make it to Beccles and back in 3 hours. With 6 hours you can go at a more leisurely pace with time for some breaks. This is a lovely, tranquil stretch of river with few large boats.

Paler blue areas of water are not open to any boats.

1 hour (approx. 3km/2 miles) Geldeston to Geldeston Lock and return
From Geldeston village paddle down the dyke and at the end turn right on to the River Waveney towards Geldeston Lock.

To Bungay
If you have a little longer you can continue towards Bungay. There are no motorboats on this stretch so it's extremely peaceful with lots of wildlife.

These maps are for illustrative purposes only and are not drawn to scale. Contains Ordnance Survey data © Crown copyright and database right 2013

Here are some suggestions for your route, whether you are paddling your own canoe or hiring one. No experience is necessary and routes are suitable for families with children. Times are approximate.

Rowan Craft, Wherry Dyke, Geldeston, Beccles NR34 0LY
01508 518208
www.rowancraft.com

If you have any problems please contact your Canoe Hire Centre. You can also contact Broads Control on 01603 756056, staffed daily 9am-6pm from April to October and 9am-5pm during the winter. If the incident is more serious please call 999 or 112 and ask for the appropriate emergency service, which may be the coastguard.

"Investing in your future"
Cross-border cooperation programme 2007-2013 Part-financed by the European Union (European Regional Development Fund)

2 Mers Seas Zeeën
INTERREG IV A

STEP

SALHOUSE BROAD CANOE TRAILS

Broads Authority
The Broads - a member of the
National Park family

Salhouse Broad, Lower Street, Salhouse NR13 6RX
01603 722775 or 07795 145475
www.salhousebroad.org.uk

The canoe hire network may make a small charge or ask for a donation for launching your own canoe.
This includes use of car parks and toilets.

Here are some suggestions for your route, whether you are paddling your own canoe or hiring one.
No experience is necessary and routes are suitable for families with children. Times are approximate and allow for breaks on the 3 hour and 6 hour trails. Please check opening times and other details for places mentioned below. **www.enjoythebroads.com**

1 hour – Explore Salhouse Broad

- Salhouse Broad on the **River Bure** is a great place to try canoeing for the first time. Explore the sheltered broad and its peaceful old **cut**, once used by sailing wherries. Find the gun boat dating back to World War I and discover hidden corners that you can only get to by canoe.
- The surrounding wet woodland known as carr, the marshland and the broad itself are home to a rich variety of wildlife including birds such as herons, great crested grebes, kingfishers, reed warblers and marsh harriers. You'll see lots of silver birch and alder trees, and in early summer you'll see yellow flag irises. Butterflies to look out for in summer include the rare swallowtail, as well as painted ladies and orange tips, and there are lots of dragonflies too such as the rare Norfolk hawker.

3 hours – Salhouse Broad to Horning
and return *(1 hour each way and 1 hour for breaks)*

- If you want to walk round the lovely and hidden away **Hoveton Great Broad Nature Trail** allow about half an hour, and there's an entrance charge. It's just across the river and is only accessible by boat.
- Practise your steering as you cross Salhouse Broad and then for Horning turn right on to the River Bure. You'll see alder carr, a mixture of willows, dog roses and great willowherb along the banks. Watch out for the low flying kingfishers on the quiet stretches round the first two bends.

- On your left you'll see **Dydall's** (or Dydler's) **Mill**, an old tower mill used for drainage. A dydler was someone who kept the dykes or narrow waterways clear. A little further on the left is the entrance to **Hoveton Little Broad** or Blackhorse Broad – paddle in for a visit and it's a good place to enjoy a picnic on the water too.
- The landscape changes as you approach Horning, the banks becoming marshy with tall reeds. Listen out for small warblers amongst the reeds.
- As you arrive at Horning you'll see the **Swan Inn** straight ahead of you. If you keep going round the meander to the right you'll come to the next pub, the **New Inn** and then the **Ferry Inn**, opposite **Woodbastwick Staithe**.
- This staithe is a starting point for the boardwalk to **Cockshoot Dyke and Broad** through part of the **Bure Marshes National Nature Reserve** – allow about three quarters of an hour there and back. A little further along the river from Woodbastwick Staithe you'll come to Cockshoot Dyke on the right. You can also take the boardwalk from here – allow about half an hour there and back. In early summer Cockshoot Dyke is one of the best places to see white water lilies. That's about your limit in 3 hours!

6 hours – Salhouse Broad to Ranworth
and return *(up to 3 hours each way, with a break)*

- From Cockshoot Dyke follow the meandering river and pass the moorings for **St Benedict's Church** on the left. Continue until you reach a turning on the right signposted for Ranworth. As you enter **Malthouse Broad** you'll see Norfolk Wildlife Trust's **Broads Wildlife Centre** and **Ranworth Broad**.
- Head straight across Malthouse Broad towards **Ranworth Staithe** moorings. There's a small **dyke** where you can leave the canoe. Visit the **information centre** here for details about the area, the Granary Shop for an ice cream or snacks and the **Maltsters** for refreshments.
- You can take a boardwalk back out to the wildlife centre and you can visit **St Helen's Church** for one of the best views in the Broads. After the 89 uneven steps, two ladders, trapdoor and vertiginous view you'll be needing a cup of tea at least, so nip into the St Helen's visitor centre and tea room to recover before you paddle back to Salhouse.

the Broads
Britain's magical waterland

Love the Broads

If you have any problems please contact your Canoe Hire Centre. You can also contact Broads Control on 01603 756056, staffed daily 9am-6pm from April to October and 9am-5pm during the winter. If the incident is more serious please call 999 or 112 and ask for the appropriate emergency service, which may be the coastguard.

www.enjoythebroads.com

Broads Authority
The Broads – a member of the National Park family

N

A1062

3 hours (approx. 7km/6 miles) Salhouse Broad to Horning and return (1 hour each way and 1 hour for breaks)

NO DAY HIRE CANOES BEYOND THIS POINT

R. Bure

Ranworth Marshes

Ranworth Dam

St Benedict's Church

Malthouse Broad

The Maltsters

dyke

WC
P

HORNING

Hobbs Mill

Ranworth Broad

Broads Wildlife Centre

St Helen's Church

RANWORTH

Ferry Inn

New Inn

Swan Inn

WC
P

Cockshoot Dyke

Woodbastwick Fens and Marshes

Cockshoot Broad Nature Reserve

Cockshoot Broad

Woodbastwick Road

STEP

"Investing in your future"
Crossborder cooperation programme
2007-2013 Part-financed by the European Union
(European Regional Development Fund)

2 Mers Seas Zeeën
INTERREG IV A

6 hours (approx. 17km/10 miles) Salhouse Broad to Ranworth and return (up to 3 hours each way, with a break)

If you have any problems please contact your Canoe Hire Centre. You can also contact Broads Control on 01603 756056, staffed daily 9am–6pm from April to October and 9am–5pm during the winter. If the incident is more serious please call 999 or 112 and ask for the appropriate emergency service, which may be the coastguard.

These maps are for illustrative purposes only and are not drawn to scale. Contains Ordnance Survey data © Crown copyright and database right 2013

1 hour
Explore Salhouse Broad
Salhouse Broad on the River Bure is a great place to try canoeing for the first time. Explore the sheltered broad and its peaceful old cut, once used by sailing wherries.

✳ Please note, the walk from the car park to Salhouse Broad is 1/3 mile/0.5km.

Here are some suggestions for your route, whether you are paddling your own canoe or hiring one. No experience is necessary and routes are suitable for families with children. Times are approximate.

A1062

HOVETON

R. Bure

Hoveton Little Broad

Bure Marshes National Nature Reserve

Decoy Broad

Dydall's Mill

Hoveton Marshes

Sedge Fen

Nature Reserve

Hoveton Great Broad

SALHOUSE BROAD

camping by permission

WC P

cut

SALHOUSE

Salhouse Road

WROXHAM

Wroxham Broad

P

Paler blue areas of water are not open to any boats.

← Wroxham

← Norwich

B1140

Canoe Hire
Salhouse Broad
01603 722775
07795 145475

KEY
● Canoe hire
● Places to get in and out

Canoe Hire Salhouse Broad,
Lower Street, Salhouse
NR13 6RX 01603 722775
or 07795 145475
www.salhousebroad.org.uk

WAYFORD BRIDGE CANOE TRAILS

Broads Authority
The Broads - a member of the
National Park family

Bank Boats, Wayford Bridge NR12 9LN
01692 582457
www.bankboats.co.uk

The canoe hire network may make a small charge or ask for a donation for launching your own canoe. This includes use of car parks and toilets.

Here are some suggestions for your route, whether you are paddling your own canoe or hiring one. No experience is necessary and routes are suitable for families with children. Times are approximate and allow for breaks. Please check opening times and other details for places mentioned below. **www.enjoythebroads.com**

For all trails
- Look out for water voles near the boatyard.

3 hours – North Walsham and Dilham Canal and return
- This is a fantastic route to choose for wildlife – there's a good chance of seeing otters and kingfishers. You should have time to explore at least part of both the left and right forks of the route.
- At the bottom of the dyke turn left on to the canal. In 1812 an Act of Parliament gave permission 'for making a navigable Canal from the Rivers Ant and Bure, at or near Wayford Bridge, near Dilham, to the towns of North Walsham and Antingham, in the county of Norfolk.' The canal allowed trading wherries to sail between North Walsham and Great Yarmouth. Very few motorised boats can use the canal so it's very peaceful.
- Where the canal forks go left for **Dilham** and the **Cross Keys Inn** for refreshments.
- Take the right fork for a jungle-like paddle. Pass under **Tonnage Bridge** and continue towards **Honing Lock**.

For all trails except North Walsham and Dilham Canal
- At the bottom of the dyke turn right on to the **River Ant**. **Hunsett Mill** on the left is a restored drainage mill.

For Stalham and Sutton
- Take the dyke to your left after the mill. This corner is a good spot for seeing otters.

3 hours – Wayford Bridge to Stalham and return
- Where the dyke forks go left for Stalham. You can moor up at **Stalham Staithe** to visit the **Museum of the Broads**. See how people's working lives shaped the landscape, and you might pass the museum's Victorian steam launch. The museum also has lots of special events.

3 hours – Wayford Bridge to Sutton and return
- Where the dyke forks go right for Sutton. You're now on **Sutton Broad** though it looks more like a dyke as the land has dried out and marsh has developed. The marshes to the south of the broad are owned by the RSPB. **Sutton Staithe Hotel** is very handy for the moorings and **Sutton Staithe Boatyard** is also a canoe hire centre.

For Neatishead (3 hours) and How Hill (6 hours)
- Continue along the River Ant. The two small dykes on your right both go to **Barton Turf**. Horatio Nelson visited his sister while she was living at Barton Turf.

3 hours – Wayford Bridge to Neatishead and return
- Continue to **Barton Broad**. Take extra care if there are strong winds on the broad. Explore the edges for a quieter and safer paddle. You'll also see more wildlife this way. Barton is the second largest broad and is a Norfolk Wildlife Trust nature reserve. It was also the site of the Broads Authority's Clear Water 2000 project – look out for otters, and water birds such as grebes, ducks, swans, moorhens coots, geese, herons and cormorants.
- Turn right for Neatishead – you can drop into the **White Horse** for refreshments, and the village also has a community shop.

6 hours – Wayford Bridge to How Hill and return
- Continue through the broad, past Pleasure Hill – in the past this was a more substantial island, popular for musical events and picnics.
- Carry on down the river and you'll see two drainage mills on the left – **Clayrack Mill** and **Boardman's Mill**. **Turf Fen Mill** is just downstream on the right. This is **How Hill National Nature Reserve** – you're almost at the moorings. Here you can enjoy one of the best views in the Broads. Visit tiny **Toad Hole Cottage**, once the home of an eel-catcher, and now a mini museum and information centre. Take the nature trail or walk along the river to **Buttle Marsh** (buttle was an old name for the rare bittern). If you have time and you want a change from paddling, there's also a guided water trail by electric boat. How Hill is a good place to see marsh harriers, and damselflies and dragonflies love the small dykes. In June and August it's one of the best places to see huge and rare swallowtail butterflies. You can also visit the How Hill Trust's Secret Gardens and sample the cakes in the tea room.
- If you have time to spare, you can carry on along the River Ant towards Ludham Bridge.

If you have any problems please contact your Canoe Hire Centre. You can also contact Broads Control on 01603 756056, staffed daily 9am-6pm from April to October and 9am-5pm during the winter. If the incident is more serious please call 999 or 112 and ask for the appropriate emergency service, which may be the coastguard.

SUTTON STAITHE CANOE TRAILS

Broads Authority
The Broads - a member of the
National Park family

Sutton Staithe Boatyard, Sutton Staithe,
Sutton NR12 9QS 01692 581653
www.suttonstaitheboatyard.co.uk

The canoe hire network may make a small charge or ask
for a donation for launching your own canoe.
This includes use of car parks and toilets.

Here are some suggestions for your route, whether you
are paddling your own canoe or hiring one.
No experience is necessary and routes are suitable for
families with children. Times are approximate and allow
for breaks. Please check opening times and other details
for places mentioned below. **www.enjoythebroads.com**

For all trails

Head straight ahead along what looks like a dyke. In
fact you're on **Sutton Broad** - it looks more like a dyke
as the land has dried out and marsh has developed.
The marshes to the south of the broad are owned by
the RSPB.

3 hours – Sutton Staithe to Stalham and return

- Where Sutton Broad joins a large dyke turn right for
  Stalham.
- You can moor up at **Stalham Staithe** to visit the
  Museum of the Broads. See how people's working
  lives shaped the landscape, and you might pass the
  museum's Victorian steam launch. The museum also
  has lots of special events.

3 hours – Sutton Staithe to Wayford Bridge and return

- For Wayford Bridge, continue along the large dyke until
  you reach the River Ant and then turn right. This corner
  is a good spot for seeing otters.
- You'll see **Hunsett Mill**, a restored drainage mill, on
  the right.
- As you approach Wayford Bridge look out water voles
  near the boatyard. **Bank Boats** is also a canoe hire
  centre.
- If you have more time you can continue under the
  bridge to explore the North Walsham and Dilham Canal
  – a good route for a quiet paddle with lots of wildlife.

For Neatishead and How Hill

- When you reach the River Ant turn left. The two small
  dykes on your right both go to **Barton Turf**.
  Horatio Nelson visited his sister while she was living
  at Barton Turf.

3 hours – Sutton Staithe to Neatishead and return

- Continue to **Barton Broad**. Take extra care if there are
  strong winds on the broad. Explore the edges for a
  quieter and safer paddle. You'll also see more wildlife
  this way. Barton is the second largest broad and is a
  Norfolk Wildlife Trust nature reserve. It was also the site
  of the Broads Authority's Clear Water 2000 project – look
  out for otters, and water birds such as grebes, ducks,
  swans, coots, moorhens, geese, herons and cormorants.
- Turn right for Neatishead – you can drop into the **White
  Horse** for refreshments, and the village also has a
  community shop.

6 hours – Sutton Staithe to How Hill and return

- Continue through the broad, past Pleasure Hill – in
  the past this was a more substantial island, popular
  for musical events and picnics.
- Carry on down the river and you'll see two drainage
  mills on the left – **Clayrack Mill** and **Boardman's Mill.**
- **Turf Fen Mill** is just downstream on the right. This is
  How Hill National Nature Reserve – you're almost at
  the moorings. Here you can enjoy one of the best views
  in the Broads. Visit tiny **Toad Hole Cottage**, once the
  home of an eel-catcher, and now a mini museum and
  information centre. Take the nature trail or walk along
  the river to **Buttle Marsh** (buttle was an old name for
  the rare bittern). If you have time and you want a
  change from paddling, there's also a guided water trail
  by electric boat. How Hill is a good place to see marsh
  harriers, and damselflies and dragonflies love the small
  dykes. In June and August it's one of the best places to
  see huge and rare swallowtail butterflies.
- You can also visit the How Hill Trust's Secret Gardens
  and sample the cakes in the tea room.
- If you have time to spare, you can carry on along the
  River Ant towards Ludham Bridge.

If you have any problems please contact your Canoe Hire Centre. You can also contact Broads Control on 01603 756056,
staffed daily 9am-6pm from April to October and 9am-5pm during the winter. If the incident is more serious please call
999 or 112 and ask for the appropriate emergency service, which may be the coastguard.

WAYFORD BRIDGE AND SUTTON STAITHE CANOE TRAILS

HONING

Honing Lock

Cross Keys Inn

Tyler's Cut

DILHAM

North Walsham and Dilham Canal

Tonnage Bridge

Broad Fen

Wayford Bridge Inn

WAYFORD BRIDGE

Here are some suggestions for your route, whether you are paddling your own canoe or hiring one. No experience is necessary and routes are suitable for families with children. Times are approximate.

Broads Authority
The Broads - a member of the National Park family

N

STALHAM

Museum of the Broads

WC

SUTTON

Stalham Staithe

Stalham Dyke

Sutton Staithe Hotel

A149

A149

← Norwich

A1151

P

Canoe Hire
Bank Boats
01692 582457

R. Ant

Barton Fen

Hunsett Mill

Sutton Broad

3 hours *(approx. 7.5km/4.6 miles)*
Wayford Bridge to Honing Lock and return

2–3 hours *(approx. 3.5km/2 miles)*
Wayford Bridge to Tyler's Cut and return

BARTON TURF

P

Canoe Hire
Sutton Staithe
01692 581653

3 hours *(approx. 9km/6 miles)*
Wayford Bridge to Stalham Staithe and return

3 hours *(approx. 9km/6 miles)*
Wayford Bridge to Sutton Staithe and return

White Horse

NEATISHEAD

P WC

Paler blue areas of water are not open to any boats.

These maps are for illustrative purposes only and are not drawn to scale.

BARTON BROAD
This is the second largest broad so it's open to winds which can affect paddling. Keep to the sides protected by reeds. If in difficulty please see the emergency details below.

Barton Broad

IRSTEAD

Clayrack Mill
Boardman's Mill

WC
i Toad Hole
Cottage Museum

HOW HILL
P

6 hours *(approx. 16.5km/10 miles)*
Wayford Bridge or Sutton Staithe to How Hill and return

If you have longer...
continue along the River Ant to Ludham Bridge.

Reedham Marsh

Turf Fen

KEY
● Canoe hire
● Places to get in and out

How Hill National Nature Reserve

Turf Fen Mill

www.enjoythebroads.com
Contains Ordnance Survey data © Crown copyright and database right 2013

R. Ant

Buttle Marsh and Ludham Bridge

If you have any problems please contact your Canoe Hire Centre. You can also contact Broads Control on 01603 756056, staffed daily 9am-6pm from April to October and 9am-5pm during the winter. If the incident is more serious please call 999 or 112 and ask for the appropriate emergency service, which may be the coastguard.

Bank Boats, Wayford Bridge NR12 9LN 01692 582457 www.bankboats.co.uk

STEP

2 Mers Seas Zeeën
INTERREG IV A

"Investing in your future"
Crossborder cooperation programme
2007-2013 Part-financed by the European Union
(European Regional Development Fund)

ADVICE TO HELP YOU ENJOY THE TRAILS

Broads Authority
The Broads - a member of the
National Park family

Planning your trip…

- Wear bright clothing for high visibility and footwear which will protect your feet.
- Things to take in a waterproof bag (provided) to go in the canoe:

  charged mobile phone

  first aid kit and antiseptic wipes

  torch and spare batteries

  waterproof clothes and spare warm clothes

  sun screen, sun hat and sunglasses

  hot and cold drinks plus lunch or snacks

  anything you need to protect such as a camera

At the launch site…

- Everyone must always wear a buoyancy aid when on or near the water. Don't remove it until you have left the water's edge.
- Beware of Weil's disease (leptospirosis) – it is very rare but serious. Cover all cuts and grazes with waterproof plasters.

On the water…

- Canoes are light and easy to tip over. Keep the canoe balanced at all times. Step into the middle when getting in and out. Sit or kneel in the canoe – don't stand up or change places unless you can hold on to the bank. Don't lean over and don't hit the bank.
- Stay on the right hand side of the river or channel. Don't cut corners on bends. Keep close to the banks unless advised otherwise.
- Keep track of time – allow enough time for the return journey. Make allowances for winds and currents which may slow you down.
- Paddle gently and at a distance from wildlife to minimise disturbance.
- Keep a lookout for other boats and anglers and give them plenty of room – they may not have seen you.
- Be considerate when entering other designated water sports zones.
- Keep clear of overhanging trees and branches.
- Don't grab hold of ropes from other boats, even if moored.
- For safety reasons don't drink alcohol on the water.
- Clean your hands with antiseptic wipes before eating or drinking.
- Never enter the water to rescue someone – reach, or throw a rope or anything that will float.
- If you capsize stay with the canoe – it will float. Swim with it to the bank, empty it out and use it to collect anything lost overboard.

And if you have your own canoe…

- Make sure your equipment, including a buoyancy aid for everyone, is suitable and in good order.
- Let someone know where you are going and when you are safely off the water.
- Take into account the weather forecast, tides, and water flows and levels in relation to your equipment and your ability, and that of others if you are in a group.
- Don't cause an obstruction when parking or obstruct footpaths with gear.
- Make sure you have permission to use the launch site and use the designated paths.
- Launch and land with care and where the bank has vegetation.

We need to minimise the spread of invasive alien species such as *Dikerogammarus villosus* or the 'killer shrimp'. So after canoeing please remember to:

Check equipment and clothing for live organisms – particularly in areas that are damp or hard to inspect. If you come across any killer shrimp, leave them at the water body where you found them.

Clean and wash all equipment, footwear and clothing thoroughly.

Dry all equipment and clothing – killer shrimp can live for up to two weeks in moist conditions. Make sure you don't transfer water to another place.

www.checkcleandry.com

EMERGENCY INFORMATION:

If you have any problems please contact your Canoe Hire Centre. You can also contact Broads Control on 01603 756056, staffed daily 9am-6pm from April to October and 9am-5pm during the winter. If the incident is more serious please call 999 or 112 and ask for the appropriate emergency service, which may be the coastguard.

BROADS AUTHORITY CANOE TRAILS

Index